Based in Somerset, Jane Tibbs has a background in education, having been a teacher and head teacher before moving into church ministry in 1999. She has a wide experience of primary school teaching and has taught music and drama in secondary schools. She was also the head of a multi-national school in Saudi Arabia, and has worked in the Falklands. Since leaving teaching, she has continued to be involved with schools as a governor and as a SIAS inspector.

Training has played a key role in Jane's work over recent years, with the provision of training courses for people who work with children in the predominantly voluntary sector of education. She has contributed to education courses for clergy and ministers in training. She is also an accredited Godly Play teacher. Jane runs a variety of workshops in churches and schools and has experience of the planning and leading of festivals and large events. Her workshops are lively and interactive. She also leads an annual holiday club and summer camp for children.

As a writer, Jane has compiled a number of resources for churches and schools to support the church's year from Advent to All Souls. She also contributes to ROOTS magazine and produces Young Church Mag, the weekly puzzle sheet for children.

Barnabas
for
Children®

Barnabas for Children ® is a registered word mark and the logo is a registered device mark of The Bible Reading Fellowship.

Text copyright © Jane Tibbs 2011
The author asserts the moral right
to be identified as the author of this work

Published by
The Bible Reading Fellowship
15 The Chambers, Vineyard
Abingdon OX14 3FE
United Kingdom
Tel: +44 (0)1865 319700
Email: enquiries@brf.org.uk
Website: www.brf.org.uk
BRF is a Registered Charity

ISBN 978 1 84101 856 0

First published 2011
10 9 8 7 6 5 4 3 2 1 0

Acknowledgments
Scripture quotations are taken from the Contemporary English Version of the Bible published by HarperCollins Publishers, copyright © 1991, 1992, 1995 American Bible Society.

Extracts from The Book of Common Prayer of 1662, the rights of which are vested in the Crown in perpetuity within the United Kingdom, are reproduced by permission of Cambridge University Press, Her Majesty's Printers.

A catalogue record for this book is available from the British Library

Printed in Singapore by Craft Print International Ltd

Creative Ideas for
Advent
&
Christmas

80 seasonal activities for the
church, home and local community

Jane Tibbs

To Joan and Peter—the best of parents,
who set me on the right road

Acknowledgments

Thank you to all my friends, colleagues and acquaintances who have patiently tolerated and experimented with my ideas over the years.

Photocopy permission

The right to photocopy material in *Creative Ideas for Advent and Christmas* is granted for the pages that contain the photocopying clause, 'Reproduced with permission from *Creative Ideas for Advent and Christmas* published by BRF 2011 (9781841018560)', so long as reproduction is for use in a teaching situation by the original purchaser. The right to photocopy material is not granted for anyone other than the original purchaser without written permission from BRF.

The Copyright Licensing Agency (CLA)

If you are resident in the UK and you have a photocopying licence with the Copyright Licensing Agency (CLA), please check the terms of your licence. If your photocopying request falls within the terms of your licence, you may proceed without seeking further permission. If your request exceeds the terms of your CLA licence, please contact the CLA direct with your request. Copyright Licensing Agency, 90 Tottenham Court Road, London W1T 4LP. Telephone 020 7631 5555; fax 020 7631 5500; email cla@cla.co.uk; website www.cla.co.uk. The CLA will provide photocopying authorisation and royalty fee information on behalf of BRF.

BRF is a Registered Charity (No. 233280)

Contents

Creative ideas for the countdown to Christmas

Creative ideas for Advent and Christmas prayers

Creative uses for Christmas cards

Creative ideas for Christmas decorations

Creative ideas for party games

Creative ideas for worship at home

Creative ideas for special saints

Appendix One

Appendix Two

Foreword

The light of candles, the scent of pine, the sight of the crib, and the expectation of Christmas are all evocative. In a world that thinks more about Santa than Jesus, and the worth of a gift rather than its significance, Jane Tibbs' book, *Creative Ideas for Advent and Christmas*, offers us a truly life-giving way of preparing for the Saviour Who Comes.

Here is a book so packed with ideas and creativity that it is a veritable feast in itself. Those who act upon its many suggestions will arrive at the Christmas season enriched and empowered. Here in a kaleidoscopic potpourri of possibilities is the story of a people preparing and celebrating. Here are possibilities for community as well as church, providing opportunities for those who think that the Christmas message needs to be heard more widely and its truth experienced more fully by all who are made in God's image.

Jane has offered us something of herself, her wisdom and imagination. It is a real gift. Why not take it as a gift to be shared, so that all—young, old, rich, poorer, believer, doubter, whoever—may find true joy in rediscovering the truth of the Christ-gift from God, born in a manger, welcomed by simple and wise alike, offering hope, love, forgiveness and peace.

+*Peter Price*
Bishop of Bath and Wells

*

Introduction

It's that time of year again! The time of year to start preparing for Christmas. The time of year to try to engage and inspire children to focus their attention on the fact that Christmas is about God sending his Son, Jesus, as a tiny baby, into the world to be its Saviour.

The four weeks before Christmas are known as the season of Advent. Advent means 'coming', so it's the time when we prepare for the coming of Jesus into the world.

The weeks before Christmas soon get clogged with preparations for the great day, which almost the whole world recognises as an occasion for parties, gestures of friendship and a holiday. For Christians, it is a time when we can prepare our hearts and lives to celebrate the birth of Jesus.

In the Bible we read, 'God loved the people of this world so much that he gave his only Son, so that everyone who has faith in him will have eternal life and never really die' (John 3:16). We remember that God gave his greatest gift to the world in Jesus, by giving presents to our friends and relations.

Nobody knows the exact date of Jesus' birthday but Pope Julius I decreed, in the third century, that Christmas Day would be 25 December. Everyone was quite happy to agree with this, as midwinter was already a time of feasting and merrymaking.

Christmas literally means the Mass of Christ and is sometimes still written as 'Christmass'.

How to use this book

Christmas is a family time and the preceding weeks of Advent offer ideal opportunities to organise family activities. Children especially like to feel involved, and organising just a few minutes each day to gather around a crib can enrich the whole meaning of Christmas.

This book offers a wealth of practical Christmassy ideas that can easily be used in church services, children's groups, together time at home, and community events in the half-term before Christmas. All the ideas use easy-to-find materials and have instant appeal. Many can be slotted into any situation, used to illustrate the story of God's plan of salvation, or just done for pure enjoyment as part of the exciting 'getting ready' time in the weeks before Christmas. Some use seasonal objects that are easy to find in the shops, such as paper chains, or things that many people will have in their Christmas box, such as last year's Christmas cards.

In total, there are 80 innovative ideas—ideal for all those needing to inspire and resource children and adults of all ages at this busy time of year. Many of the ideas could become annual events, woven into the tradition of the church, home or local community.

Creative ideas for the local community

Advent is a special time of year that stirs the imagination and kindles memories, a season of preparation and promise that culminates in the celebration of Christmas Day. Perhaps no other time captures the imagination quite like the run-up to Christmas, and many people who would not normally dream of attending a church service find themselves happily singing Christmas hymns and carols and listening to the nativity story at some point during the season.

With many people also in party mode, the weeks of Advent offer an ideal opportunity to hold some events for people in the local community to enjoy.

❄ ✳ ❄

— Posada —

You will need:

The characters of Mary, Joseph and a donkey from a set of nativity crib figures

Crib figures can be made of wood or other traditional materials. They might be the figures normally used in your church at Christmas or they could be specially made for the event. Some communities have made extra-large or even life-size models of the figures: the possibilities are as great as your imagination and the skills and materials you have at your disposal.

An effective way of linking the traditional readings for Advent with the themes of preparation, concern for others and spiritual readiness is by adapting the Mexican custom of the Posada.

Posada means 'hospitality', 'inn' or 'place of shelter'. It is an old custom, probably introduced into Latin America by Spanish friars. The ritual focuses on two of the Gospel themes for the season: the rejection of Joseph and Mary by the innkeepers at Bethlehem (representing the rejection of unpopular demands for righteous living) and joy at the birth of Jesus (representing the joy that comes from welcoming and accepting God into our lives).

Homes willing to host the nativity figures are chosen and, one evening early in Advent, a group of worshippers carrying figures of Mary, Joseph and a donkey gathers at one of the houses.

Host families will want to decorate their homes and perhaps invite neighbours in. They might like to have a piñata filled with sweets and nuts for children to break at the end of the evening. (See page 126 for instructions on how to make a piñata.)

After keeping the nativity figures for one night or more (depending on how many families are taking part), each host family then takes the figures to the next house in procession. When they arrive at the designated house, they knock at the door of the host and a dialogue between the new host and the visiting guests takes place. The dialogue can be extended a little if required, but a basic script is given below.

Host: Who knocks at my door so late?
Procession: Open, please open! We need shelter for the
            night.
Host: Go away! Don't disturb us! We don't know you.
Procession: We have come very far. I am Joseph, and Mary is
            with me. She is going to give birth to God's Son.
Host: Gladly, gladly we welcome you to our humble
            home. Welcome, Mary! Welcome, Joseph!
            Welcome, good pilgrims!

Hosts pray: O God, give us grace to cast away darkness and put on the armour of light in this life, in which your Son Jesus Christ came to visit us in great humility; that when he comes again to judge both the quick and the dead, we may rise to life immortal, through him. Amen

Bible reading: Psalm 90

Conclusion: The processional dialogue ends with the singing of a couple of carols of the host's choice.

On Christmas Eve, the figures of Mary and Joseph are carried to the church and placed in the stable, perhaps as part of a crib service.

Alongside the wooden figures for Mary, Joseph and the donkey, the procession can be brought to life by inviting children to dress up for the event. For each host family taking part in the Posada, one child needs to be Mary and another Joseph. You could also choose someone to dress as the donkey, with a simple costume and a donkey mask. Other children can dress up as different people. Perhaps they could be people who are often rejected, or other characters from the Christmas story. Or perhaps it could be an occasion for dressing up in different national costumes to represent the message of Christmas going out to the world.

The Posada needs to be adapted to suit local conditions. Ensure that there is enough adult supervision and that members of the church community know they will be visited. Walk with the children around part of the village or town, singing carols. At the homes of the chosen church members, ask the children playing the roles of Mary and Joseph to knock on the door and ask for a room for the night. The church members need to act as the belligerent innkeepers who will reject the group.

On Christmas Eve, the group finally arrives at the church, where they are welcomed with open arms by the congregation. There can be a short service or a blessing of the crib (see page 109 for a sample liturgy). The joy of Christmas is celebrated and the children are welcomed again in the Christian community. The service can be followed by a party.

❊ ✱ ❊

— Christmas tree festival —

You will need:

A Christmas tree for each organisation taking part; printed materials to publicise the event, give details of what is required and provide a programme for visitors; registration cards; display cards naming the charities nominated for each tree; a bowl or basket for each tree; refreshments for the festival day itself; Christmas gifts stall (optional)

A Christmas tree festival is an excellent idea to involve the whole community in a bit of tree decorating. The event is not difficult to organise but pre-planning is needed to ensure that everything is decided well in advance of the event itself. Things to consider are listed below.

Local businesses, schools and individuals are asked to decorate a Christmas tree, and the trees are all displayed in the church for people to come and admire. A charity is nominated for each tree by the decorators and visitors choose their favourites by putting a few small coins in a bowl or basket in front of each tree. The money is then donated to the charity.

To make it more than just a collection of Christmas trees, have refreshments available and perhaps include a sale of Christmas gifts and goodies. A carol service could be an added attraction.

- Decide on the date for your festival.
- Decide the size of the trees to decorated.

- Order the trees from a local supplier (as early in the year as possible).
- Decide whether the festival will support just one charity or whether each tree will be for a different charity.
- Choose a theme for your festival, or leave it up to the contributors to decorate their tree in a way that reflects their organisation.

In September, invite local organisations to take part in the festival. You will need to charge a small registration fee to cover the cost of the trees. In November, send out details of the times for decorating the trees to all participants and print a programme for visitors. In December, enjoy the display.

❄ ✳ ❄

— Nativity scene festival —

You will need:

Tables and portable or fixed display units; plain fabric sheeting or tablecloths; plain card or paper for labelling the displays; permanent marker pens; Luke 2:1–7 and Luke 2:8–20 printed out on display cards

Many people have nativity scenes that they carefully put on display every Christmas, and it's surprising how many families collect nativity scenes from around the world. These scenes can be put to good use during the weeks before Christmas by having a nativity scene festival.

Decide on the most suitable venue, such as a side chapel in your church building, a church hall, a local community centre or a school, to hold such an event. Invite people to retrieve their nativity scenes from their storage place a little earlier than usual. Ensure that the display area is well prepared; perhaps cover all the tables and display units in the same plain fabric to show the scenes to their best advantage.

People may like to write a few lines about their own nativity scene. If so, it would be a good idea to coordinate the presentation by ensuring that the same paper and backing cards are used for them all.

Print out the familiar verses from Luke 2:1–7 (the birth of Jesus) and Luke 2:8–20 (the visit of the angels to the shepherds) in various translations, and display them around the exhibition area. If there are some foreign nativity scenes, the verses could be printed in the appropriate language (use the internet to find a website, such as www.biblegateway.com, that can supply a correct translation).

Take the opportunity to provide refreshments for visitors and, perhaps, get children and adults alike involved in a make-your-own-nativity workshop. You could give the workshop a title, such as 'DIY Nativity'. Provide art and craft materials, wipe-clean covering for tables and an allocated space for the finished nativities to be displayed.

The exhibition could be opened or closed with a crib service (see page 115 for a sample liturgy). After the event, it may be possible to encourage people who have windows that can be seen easily from the street to put a tree from the festival display in their window for everyone to see.

— Village or town nativity —

You will need to choose the scenes you want to illustrate, select your characters and locations, and make the costumes and props. For example:

Characters

- Isaiah (messianic prophecies)
- Mary and the angel Gabriel (annunciation)

- Mary and Joseph (nativity)
- Shepherds and angels (proclamation)
- Wise men (Epiphany)

Locations

- Church building
- Private garages or similar
- Community buildings (village or town hall or local school)

This is a way of taking the nativity story around a community. It works well in a small community. For example, one village with just 54 properties, which were mostly clustered in an area surrounding the village green, put on such an event.

If you have a village hall, you could turn it into a 'Nobody Inn' and make refreshments continually available, such as mince pies, Christmas cakes, mulled wine, tea, coffee and squash.

The characters in each scene need to know their part of the story so that they can answer any questions. Also, a quiz for the children will help them make the most of their trip around the nativity. (See pages 25–29 for sample quiz questions.)

Identify a starting place for people to begin their journey around the different scenes and provide them with a map of the route. It may also be advisable to have stewards along the route so that people don't get lost. You may also find it necessary to inform the local police so that any necessary traffic restrictions can be put in place.

Isaiah

Choose a venue, such as a special area in the local church, for Isaiah to sit in splendour. Dress the character in flowing robes and, if possible, complete the look with an enormous grey beard. Write out the following Bible passages on card, so that they can be displayed in the area. Isaiah can also recite the prophecies to those who visit.

Those who walked in the dark have seen a bright light. And it shines upon everyone who lives in the land of darkest shadows.

ISAIAH 9:2

A child has been born for us. We have been given a son who will be our ruler. His names will be Wonderful Adviser and Mighty God, Eternal Father and Prince of Peace. His power will never end; peace will last for ever. He will rule David's kingdom and make it grow strong. He will always rule with honesty and justice. The Lord All-Powerful will make certain that all of this is done.

ISAIAH 9:6–7

Like a branch that sprouts from a stump, someone from David's family will some day be king. The Spirit of the Lord will be with him to give him understanding, wisdom, and insight. He will be powerful, and he will know and honour the Lord. His greatest joy will be to obey the Lord. This king won't judge by appearances or listen to rumours. The poor and the needy will be treated with fairness and with justice. His word will be law everywhere in the land… Honesty and fairness will be his royal robes.

Leopards will lie down with young goats, and wolves will rest with lambs. Calves and lions will eat together and be cared for by little children. Cows and bears will share the same pasture; their young will rest side by side. Lions and oxen will both eat straw… Nothing harmful will take place on the Lord's holy mountain. Just as water fills the sea, the land will be filled with people who know and honour the Lord.

ISAIAH 11:1–7, 9

Mary and the angel Gabriel

A nearby garage could be converted into a room in a Middle Eastern house for the annunciation, complete with a teenage Mary and an angel Gabriel, both in costume. Simple props might include a low table with rustic bread-making items displayed upon it, a cottage-style broom and a small wooden stool. The Bible passage could be displayed on card for visitors to read, each paragraph being written out on a separate piece of card so that there is not too much text to read at once. The Bible story could also be read out to those who visit, as a shared reading between Mary and the angel, by a third person acting as a narrator, or by playing it from a pre-recorded CD.

One month later God sent the angel Gabriel to the town of Nazareth in Galilee with a message for a virgin named Mary. She was engaged to Joseph from the family of King David. The angel greeted Mary and said, 'You are truly blessed! The Lord is with you.'

Mary was confused by the angel's words and wondered what they meant. Then the angel told Mary, 'Don't be afraid! God is pleased with you, and you will have a son. His name will be Jesus. He will be great and will be called the Son of God Most High. The Lord God will make him king, as his ancestor David was. He will rule the people of Israel for ever, and his kingdom will never end.'

Mary asked the angel, 'How can this happen? I am not married!'

The angel answered, 'The Holy Spirit will come down to you, and God's power will come over you. So your child will be called the holy Son of God. Your relative Elizabeth is also going to have a son, even though she is old. No one thought she could ever have a baby, but in three months she will have a son. Nothing is impossible for God!'

Mary said, 'I am the Lord's servant! Let it happen as you have said.' And the angel left her.

LUKE 1:26–38

Mary and Joseph

Another venue a little further away, such as a garage, could become the stable for the nativity scene. Perhaps a young couple with a new baby could be persuaded to act as the holy family. Props for the scene could include a simple manger, fashioned from a baby's crib, with bales of straw for Mary and Joseph to sit on. It is important to ensure that the building used is adequately heated for the health and comfort of the youngest member of the scene.

The Bible passage could be displayed on card for visitors to read. The Bible story could also be read out to those who visit, as a shared reading between Mary and Joseph, by a third person acting as a narrator, or by playing it from a pre-recorded CD.

About that time Emperor Augustus gave orders for the names of all the people to be listed in record books. These first records were made when Quirinius was governor of Syria. Everyone had to go to their own home town to be listed. So Joseph had to leave Nazareth in Galilee and go to Bethlehem in Judea. Long ago Bethlehem had been King David's home town, and Joseph went there because he was from David's family. Mary was engaged to Joseph and travelled with him to Bethlehem. She was soon going to have a baby, and while they were there, she gave birth to her firstborn son. She dressed him in baby clothes and laid him on a bed of hay, because there was no room for them in the inn.
LUKE 2:1–7

Shepherds and angels

If the setting is rural, it may be possible to persuade a local farmer to bring some of his sheep to the top of a field and pen them securely so that some of the teenage boys can become shepherds for the evening. Other children could play the roles of a host of angels singing. Carols such as 'While shepherds watched', 'Angels from the realms of glory' or 'Hark! The herald-angels sing' would be suitable choices for the angels to perform, or to be played from a CD. If the provision of real sheep is not an option, the scene could be set on a village green or in a local park or playing field, with the sheep made out of card flats, grouped to look like a flock.

As this scene is played out in the open, ensure that it is set adjacent to a source of light, or provide battery-powered lanterns to light the area so that the characters can be clearly seen.

The Bible passage could be displayed on card for visitors to read. The Bible story could also be read out to those who visit, as a shared reading between the shepherds and angels, by a third person acting as a narrator, or by playing it from a pre-recorded CD.

That night in the fields near Bethlehem some shepherds were guarding their sheep. All at once an angel came down to them from the Lord, and the brightness of the Lord's glory flashed around them. The shepherds were frightened. But the angel said, 'Don't be afraid! I have good news for you, which will make everyone happy. This very day in King David's home town a Saviour was born for you. He is Christ the Lord. You will know who he is, because you will find him dressed in baby clothes and lying on a bed of hay.'

Suddenly many other angels came down from heaven and joined in praising God. They said: 'Praise God in heaven! Peace on earth to everyone who pleases God.'

LUKE 2:8–14

Wise men

The wise men could be located on the edge of the village, either in another converted garage or in a house. Props for the scene should include a star, placed in such a way as to indicate that the wise men have started their journey.

The Bible passage could be displayed on card for visitors to read, each paragraph being written out on a separate piece of card so that there is not too much text to read at once. The Bible story could also be read out to those who visit, as a shared reading between the wise men, by a third person acting as a narrator, or by playing it from a pre-recorded CD.

When Jesus was born in the village of Bethlehem in Judea, Herod was king. During this time some wise men from the east came to Jerusalem and said, 'Where is the child born to be king of the Jews? We saw his star in the east and have come to worship him.'

When King Herod heard about this, he was worried, and so was everyone else in Jerusalem. Herod brought together the chief priests and the teachers of the Law of Moses and asked them, 'Where will the Messiah be born?' They told him, 'He will be born in Bethlehem, just as the prophet wrote, "Bethlehem in the land of Judea, you are very important among the towns of Judea. From your town will come a leader, who will be like a shepherd for my people Israel."'

Herod secretly called in the wise men and asked them when they had first seen the star. He told them, 'Go to Bethlehem and search carefully for the child. As soon as you find him, let me know. I want to go and worship him too.'

The wise men listened to what the king said and then left. And the star they had seen in the east went on ahead of them until it stopped over the place where the child was. They were thrilled and excited to see the star.

MATTHEW 2:1–10

Once all the visitors have completed their journey around the nativity scenes, invite everyone (including those taking part in the story) to gather in the 'Nobody Inn' for some carol singing, refreshments and a retelling of the Christmas story.

❄ ✱ ❄

— Family Christmas quiz —

You will need:

A sheet of questions; a score board; permanent markers; a microphone (optional); small prizes for the winning team and a consolation prize for the team that comes last (optional); refreshments

This is just like a quiz night but the questions are all related to Christmas and include some that the children will be able to answer.

Arrange for the quiz to take place at a suitable time for families rather than later in the evening, and ensure there is a good spread of food. Holding the event at tea-time might be a good idea. Refreshments can be eaten at the beginning, during an interval or at the end. Invite each family to contribute a certain amount to cover the costs and donate any excess to a Christmas charity.

Appoint a quizmaster and ensure that questions will be easily heard at your venue. If necessary, provide some sort of amplification.

You can choose any questions but it is a good idea to have about six sections, with eight questions in each section, so that the younger competitors don't get bored. You will need answer sheets for each family and something to write with. Families can think of an appropriate name for their team. Teams needn't be all from one family, so people who live alone can be included, but you might like to limit a team to six members with at least two children in each team.

The sections of the quiz could include the following:

- Christmas carols
- People in the Christmas story
- Christmas food
- Literary characters from books set at Christmas time
- Events that happened on Christmas Day

- Famous Christmas Day birthdays
- Christmas pictures

If you wish to provide a prize for the winning team and a consolation prize for the team that comes last, suitable choices could include boxes of sweets that can be shared (avoiding those that contain nuts), small stocking filler gifts or traditional party bag items, such as small pots of bubbles.

Sample Christmas quiz questions

Christmas carols

- Name eight reindeer apart from Rudolph.
  (Comet, Cupid, Dasher, Dancer, Prancer, Vixen, Donner, Blitzen)
- The song 'White Christmas' was first performed in which 1942 film?
  (*Holiday Inn*)
- What is the English title of the carol written in 1818 by Austrian priest Josef Mohr?
  (Silent night)
- Which tree in the woods bears the crown?
  (Holly)
- Which carol includes the words 'Bless all the dear children in your tender care'?
  (Away in a manger)
- Who do we bring good tidings to?
  (You and your kin)
- How many ships were sailing by?
  (Three)
- Who looked out on the feast of Stephen?
  (Good King Wenceslas)
- Which carol traditionally starts the service of Nine Lessons and Carols from King's College, Cambridge?
  (Once in royal David's city)

People in the Christmas story

- Who is Christmas all about?
  (Jesus)
- What was the name of his mother?
  (Mary)
- What was the name of her husband?
  (Joseph)
- What was the name of Mary's cousin, who was also going to have a baby?
  (Elizabeth)
- Who told Mary and Joseph to use the stable?
  (Innkeeper)
- Who did the angels tell about the birth of a baby in Bethlehem?
  (Shepherds)
- Who else came to visit Jesus?
  (Wise men)
- What was the name of the king who told the wise men to go and find the child and then bring him news so he could go and worship?
  (Herod)

Christmas food

- What is the name of the cake traditionally eaten in Italy at Christmas?
  (Panettone)
- What is the popular name of the little baked sausages wrapped in rashers of streaky bacon?
  (Pigs in blankets)
- Traditionally eaten in Germany, what sort of food is *Stollen*?
  (Cake)
- Which vegetable is often included in the ingredients of a Christmas pudding?
  (Carrot)

- Yorkshire man William Strickland is believed to have brought the first of these to Britain from North America in 1526.
  (Turkey)
- Which nuts are traditionally served with Christmas dinner?
  (Chestnuts)
- What is the name of the fruit sauce that traditionally accompanies the Christmas turkey?
  (Cranberry sauce)
- Which country celebrates on Christmas Eve with a meal of twelve courses to represent the twelve apostles?
  (Poland)

Literary characters

- In Charles Dickens' novel *A Christmas Carol*, who was Scrooge's dead business partner?
  (Jacob Marley)
- Who are the four ghosts in *A Christmas Carol*?
  (Christmas Past, Christmas Present, Christmas Yet to Come, Jacob Marley)
- Which Dr Zeuss character steals Christmas?
  (The Grinch)
- Which young lady said, 'Christmas won't be Christmas without any presents'?
  (Jo in *Little Women*)
- Which Dickensian character goes skating on Christmas Day and falls through the ice?
  (Mr Pickwick)
- Which animal carol singers visit Mole in *The Wind in the Willows*?
  (Mice)
- Which poet wrote a play called *Nativity*?
  (John Donne)

Events that happened at Christmas

- In which year was there a Christmas truce when British and German troops stopped fighting and sang carols?
  (1914)
- When was the first royal Christmas Day broadcast?
  (1932)
- Which British monarch made the first broadcast?
  (George V)
- When was the monarch's Christmas Day speech first televised?
  (1957)
- Which river did George Washington cross on Christmas night, 1776, during the American Revolutionary War?
  (Delaware)
- The Christmas period of 1813–14 saw the last what in London?
  (Christmas Fair on a frozen River Thames)
- Which diarist noted on Christmas Day 1662, 'Had a pleasant walk to White Hall, where I intended to receive communion with the family, but I have come too late…'?
  (Samuel Pepys)
- When was the first Christmas card sent?
  (1843)
- William the Conqueror was crowned at Westminster Abbey on Christmas Day in which year?
  (1066)

Famous Christmas Day birthdays

- This famous scientist and mathematician was born in 1642.
  (Sir Isaac Newton)
- This famous hotelier was born in 1887.
  (Conrad Hilton)
- Which Pope was born on Christmas Day in 1717?
  (Pope Pius VI)

- This female singer from Scotland was born in 1954.
  (Annie Lennox)
- On Christmas Day in which year was Kenny Everett born?
  (1944)
- Which famous model was born on Christmas day in 1968?
  (Helena Christensen)
- Which Egyptian president was born on Christmas Day in 1918?
  (Muhammad Anwar Al Sadat)
- Humphrey Bogart was born on Christmas Day in which year?
  (1899)

❄ ✦ ❄

— Christingle service —

You will need:

Christingle service sheets (see link below); small oranges; cocktail
sticks; selection of small sweets and raisins; lengths of narrow red
ribbon; small white candles; circles of white card; refreshments

If your community doesn't hold a Christingle service, it might
be a good idea to arrange one. Christingle services can be held at
any time from Advent Sunday until Candlemas, which falls on 2
February, or the Sunday nearest to that date.

All the information and ideas you need can be found on the
Children's Society website: www.childrenssociety.org.uk.

The service is best held at a time of day when families with small
children can easily be present. On a winter's afternoon, the service
is very effective if darkness is falling as the candles are lit. After the
service, you may wish to provide an opportunity for refreshments,
with space for people to meet each other, linger a while and chat.

Health and safety

Candles that are lit are an obvious safety hazard, so care must be taken to ensure that no one gets burned. Check that first aid and fire extinguishing equipment are available and that fire exits are clearly marked. Make sure there are some adult helpers who will keep a watchful eye on potential problems.

Glow candles are now available as an alternative to candle flames, and these can be viewed on the website www.glow-candles.com.

— Mummers' play —

You will need:

Copies of the script below; stage setting, props and costumes as available

Mummers' plays are among England's oldest Christmas traditions and are best described as early pantomime. In the plays, which are based loosely on the legend of George and the dragon, people dress up and act out the fight between darkness and light.

A Mummers' play is something that a whole community could work on, including references that are relevant only to the people who live there. Below is the outline of a play that can easily be enhanced and embellished to suit any community.

Have fun!

Cast

- Bold knight, dressed in black
- Sir George, dressed in white
- Doctor, dressed in green
- Father Christmas, dressed in red and white
- Little Jack, dressed in any colour

Little Jack:
> In come I, little Johnny Jack.
> I see the winter has come back,
> But rain or snow won't keep me away,
> I've come to see your mummers' play.
> Ladies and gentlemen, give what you please,
> Give it to old Father Chrissymas, please.

Father Christmas:
> In come I, Old Father Christmas,
> Welcome or welcome not,
> I hope old Father Christmas
> Will never be forgot!
> Although we've got but a short time to stay,
> We've come to show you a jolly old play.
> In comes our hero dressed in white,
> He's bold Sir George,
> yes, George the knight.

Sir George:
> In come I, St George the bold,
> Oh, I say, this country's cold.
> I've been away to warmer lands,
> Fighting a dragon with my hands.
> I at last brought him to slaughter
> And now I'll marry the king's fair daughter.

Bold knight:
> In come I. the big bold knight,
> I've nothing to do so I fancied a fight.
> I'll fight St George,
> he's supposed to be strong,
> But between you and me, he won't live long!

Reproduced with permission from *Creative Ideas for Advent and Christmas* published by BRF 2011 (978 1 84101 856 0) www.barnabasinchurches.org.uk

St George and the Bold Knight take out wooden swords and fight. The Bold Knight wins. St George falls to the ground. The audience shouts, 'Aaaah!'

Doctor: In come I, the good doctor Grub,
                 I'll wake Sir George with my strong club.

The Doctor pretends to bash George with a mallet, but actually hits the ground to make a loud thud.

Doctor: I'll sprinkle him with lots of water
                 To make him fit for the king's dear daughter.
                 I'll put some powder on his head.
                 Rise up, Sir George, you're no longer dead.

Cheers from the audience.

Father Christmas
and Little Jack: Hurray! Hurray! Our play is done,
                    Bold Knight has lost, Sir George has won,
                    We can no longer wait around here,
                    Merry Christmas and a happy New Year!

＊

Creative ideas
for Christmas cooking

Most children enjoy the food preparations for Christmas. Simple biscuits, cakes and sweets can be made and then given as gifts to friends and family.

Health and safety

If the recipes are being made in a group situation, you will need to check for food allergies and have alternative ingredients available as appropriate.

A kitchen can be a dangerous place, so when cooking with children it's a good idea to have a few rules that the children can relate to.

- If using knives, sharp ones are safer than blunt ones, but should always be used under supervision. Always carry a knife pointing downwards and pass it to someone else with the handle facing them.
- A kitchen is a fire hazard. Fire hazards include tea towels (make sure they are hung up away from the cooker), sockets (never touch with wet hands, and use socket covers) and saucepans on a hob (keep handles facing inwards). Make sure you know where the fire extinguisher is and that a fire blanket is also available.
- Wear an apron to protect from spatters.
- Cookers are very hot. Always use a dry oven glove to lift something hot and avoid touching an open oven door.
- Don't forget that steam is really hot, too.
- Always wash hands before cooking.

❄ ✶ ❄

— Star biscuits —

For 24 biscuits you will need:

- 100g (4oz) margarine
- 150g (6oz) plain flour
- 1 egg
- 75g (3oz) sugar
- 1 tsp ground cinnamon
- ½ tsp ground mixed spice

- Rolling pin and star cutters
- A baking tray, wiped with oil

Method

1. Heat the oven to 180C, 350F, gas mark 4.
2. Rub the margarine into the flour mixed with the spices. Cream the egg with the sugar and stir into the flour mixture.
3. Dust a rolling pin and a clean work surface with flour. Roll out the mixture and cut into star shapes.
4. Put the stars on a greased baking tray and bake in the oven for 15 minutes or until golden brown.
5. Allow to cool on the tray. Decorate as desired.

❄ ✶ ❄

— Cheesy Christmas stars —

For about 24 stars you will need:

- 150g (6oz) self-raising flour
- ½ tsp salt

- 75g (3oz) butter or margarine
- 75g (3oz) cheese, grated
- 1 egg and 1 tbsp milk, beaten together

- Rolling pin and star cutters
- A baking tray, wiped with oil

Method

1. Heat the oven to 200C, 400F, gas mark 6.
2. Sift the flour and salt into a bowl through a sieve. Add the butter or margarine and rub it in to make fine breadcrumbs.
3. Leave a tablespoon of the grated cheese on a saucer. Add the rest of the cheese to the bowl and stir it in.
4. Put a tablespoon of the beaten egg and milk mixture into a cup. Mix the rest into the flour to make a dough.
5. Dust a rolling pin and a clean work surface with flour. Roll out the dough until it is slightly thinner than your little finger and cut into star shapes.
6. Brush the stars with the rest of the egg mixture and sprinkle them with the rest of the cheese.
7. Put the stars on to a greased baking tray and bake in the oven for 10 minutes until they are golden.
8. Allow to cool on the tray.

❄ ✦ ❄

— Starry jam tart —

You will need:

- 350g (12oz) packet shortcrust pastry
- 2 tbsp plain flour
- 6 rounded tbsp seedless raspberry or strawberry jam
- 1 tbsp milk

- Plastic foodwrap
- 20cm (8in) flan tin
- Small star-shaped cookie cutter and rolling pin

Method

1. Heat the oven to 200C, 400F, gas mark 6.
2. Take the pastry out of the fridge and leave it for 10 minutes. Sprinkle a little of the flour over a clean work surface.
3. Cut off a quarter of the pastry and wrap it in the plastic food wrap. Sprinkle a little of the flour on to the rolling pin.
4. Roll out the bigger piece of pastry. Turn it a little and roll it again to make a circle about 30cm (12in) across.
5. Put the rolling pin at one side of the pastry, roll the pastry around it and lift it up. Then place it over the flan tin and unroll the pastry.
6. Dip your fingers into some flour and press the pastry into the edges of the tin. Then, roll the rolling pin across the top.
7. Spoon the jam into the pastry case. Spread it out with the back of a spoon.
8. Roll out the rest of the pastry. Using the cutter, cut out about 12 pastry stars. Brush them with a little milk and place them on top of the jam.
9. Bake the tart in the oven for about 20 minutes.
10. Take the tart out of the oven and let the jam cool before serving.

❄ ✳ ❄

— Chocolate truffles —

To make about ten truffles you will need:

- 100g (4oz) plain chocolate
- 25g (1oz) butter
- 25g (1oz) icing sugar

- 50g (2oz) plain cake, crumbled into fine crumbs
- 2 tbsp desiccated coconut
- 2 tbsp chocolate sugar strands

- Small paper cases

Method

1. Fill a large pan a quarter full of water and heat it until the water bubbles. Remove the pan from the heat.
2. Put the chocolate and the butter into a heatproof bowl and, wearing oven gloves, gently put the bowl in the pan.
3. Stir the chocolate and butter together until they have melted. Using oven gloves, lift the bowl out of the water.
4. Sift the icing sugar into the chocolate. Add the cake crumbs and stir everything until it is well mixed.
5. Leave the mixture to cool. Put the desiccated coconut on to one plate and the chocolate strands on to another.
6. When the mixture is firm and thick, scoop up some with a teaspoon. Put the spoonful into the coconut or strands.
7. Roll the spoonful around until it is covered, then put it in a paper case.
8. Make lots more truffles!
9. Put the truffles on to a large plate and put the plate in the fridge for 30 minutes, or until the truffles are firm.

❄ ✹ ❄

— Snowball truffles —

To make about ten truffles you will need:

- 100g (4oz) white chocolate
- 25g (1oz) butter
- 25g (1oz) icing sugar

- 50g (2oz) plain cake, crumbled into fine crumbs
- 4 tbsp desiccated coconut

- Small paper cases

Method

1. Fill a large pan a quarter full of water and heat it until the water bubbles. Remove the pan from the heat.
2. Put the chocolate and the butter into a heatproof bowl and, wearing oven gloves, gently put the bowl in the pan.
3. Stir the chocolate and butter together until they have melted. Using oven gloves, lift the bowl out of the water.
4. Sift the icing sugar into the chocolate. Add the cake crumbs and stir everything until it is well mixed.
5. Leave the mixture to cool. Put the desiccated coconut on to a plate.
6. When the mixture is firm and thick, scoop up some with a teaspoon. Put the spoonful into the coconut.
7. Roll the spoonful around until it is covered, then put it in a paper case.
8. Make lots more truffles!
9. Put the truffles on to a large plate and put the plate in the fridge for 30 minutes, or until the truffles are firm.

— Snowy meringues —

To make about 30 meringues you will need:

- 2 eggs at room temperature
- 100g (4oz) caster sugar
- Sugar sprinkles

- Two baking trays lined with baking parchment

Method

1. Heat the oven to 110C, 225F, gas mark ¼ before you start.
2. Break one of the eggs on the edge of a large bowl and pour it on to a saucer, making sure you don't break the yolk.
3. Hold an egg cup over the yolk and carefully tip the saucer over the bowl so that the egg white dribbles into it.
4. Repeat this with the second egg so that both egg whites are in the bowl. You don't need the egg yolks for this recipe (but you can save them for the next).
5. Whisk the egg whites until they are really thick. They should form stiff points when you lift the whisk up.
6. Add a tablespoon of sugar to the egg white and whisk it in. Whisk in the rest of the sugar, one tablespoon at a time.
7. Scoop up a teaspoon of the mixture, then use another teaspoon to push it off on to one of the lined baking trays.
8. When you have used all the mixture, sprinkle a few sugar sprinkles over each one.
9. Put the meringues into the oven and bake them for 40 minutes. Then turn off the oven, leaving the meringues inside.
10. After 15 minutes, carefully take the baking trays out of the oven. Leave the meringues on the trays to cool.

— Painted biscuits —

To make about 15 biscuits you will need:

- 50g (2oz) icing sugar
- 75g (3oz) soft margarine
- The yolk from a large egg (left over from snowy meringues)
- A few drops of vanilla essence
- 150g (5oz) plain flour

- Plastic food wrap
- Cookie cutters and a rolling pin
- A baking sheet, wiped with cooking oil

To decorate the biscuits:

- An egg yolk (left over from snowy meringues)
- Food colouring

Method

1. Heat the oven to 180C, 350F, gas mark 4, before you start.
2. Use a sieve to sift the icing sugar into a large bowl. Add the margarine and stir it until the mixture is smooth.
3. Stir in the egg yolk and a few drops of vanilla essence. Sift the flour through a sieve into the bowl.
4. Mix in the flour. Keep mixing until you have made a smooth dough. Wrap it in foodwrap and put it in the freezer to get cool.
5. Put the egg yolk into a bowl. Beat it with a fork and divide it between several saucers. Mix a few drops of different food colouring with each one.
6. Take the dough out of the freezer. Sprinkle some flour over a rolling pin and clean work surface. Roll out the dough.
7. Keep rolling out the dough until it is as thin as your little finger.
8. Use the cutters to press shapes out of the dough. Roll out the leftover dough and cut out more shapes. Use a spatula to lift them on to the oiled baking tray.
9. Use a clean paintbrush to paint shapes and patterns on to the biscuits with the mixtures of egg and food colouring.
10. Bake the biscuits for 10–12 minutes.
11. Take them out of the oven (wearing oven gloves) and let them cool. Lift them on to a wire rack.

❄ ✳ ❄

— Candle cakes —

You will need:

- 12 small sponge cakes (available in a supermarket)
- 175g (6oz) icing sugar
- 2 tbsp lemon juice
- 100g (4oz) seedless raspberry or strawberry jam
- Small sweets and sugar strands

- 12 birthday cake candles and holders

Method

1. If necessary, take the cakes out of the cake cases. Turn each cake on its side and cut it in half. Spread the jam on the bottom half and lay the top half back on top.
3. Sift the icing sugar into a bowl. Mix in the lemon juice and a little water if necessary.
3. Spoon the icing on to the cakes and press on some sweets and sprinkles.
4. Push a candle into the top of each cake.

❄ ✳ ❄

— Coconut Christmas mice —

To make about 12 large mice you will need:

- 250g (9oz) icing sugar, sifted
- 200g (8oz) tin of condensed milk
- 175g (7oz) desiccated coconut
- Red food colouring

- Sweets for ears
- Silver cake-decorating balls
- Liquorice 'bootlaces' or thick yarn

- Plastic foodwrap

Method

1. Mix the icing sugar and the condensed milk together in a bowl. Mix in the coconut and divide the mixture between two bowls.
2. Add a few drops of red colouring to each bowl and mix it in. Then add a few more drops of colouring to one of the bowls to make a darker shade.
3. For a body, dip a spoon into some warm water and let it drip a little. Then, lift out a big spoonful of the mixture from either one of the bowls.
4. Pat the spoonful smooth on top. Turn the spoon over and carefully drop the shape on to a piece of plastic foodwrap.
5. Pinch the thinner end of the shape to make a nose. Then, carefully press the sweets and silver balls into the body for the ears and eyes.
6. Push a piece of liquorice or thick yarn under the body for a tail. Leave the mouse to harden on a plate.
7. Make more mice.

— Peep-hole sandwiches —

To make three rounds of sandwiches you will need:

- 6 slices of bread
- Butter or margarine
- Thin slices of ham

- A cucumber
- Strawberry, raspberry or apricot jam

- A large round cookie cutter
- Small, shaped cookie cutter

Method

1. Lay a slice of bread on a chopping board. Cut out a circle using the round cutter and remove the circle.
2. Cut another circle from a second slice of bread. Then, using a shaped cutter, cut a small shape in one of the circles.
3. Lay the round cutter on top of a slice of ham and carefully cut around the cutter with a sharp knife.
4. Butter one side of each bread circle. Lay the ham on the whole circle and lay the circle with the hole on top.
5. Cut another two bread circles and cut a hole in one of them. Slice the cucumber until you have lots of thin slices.
6. Butter the bread circles and lay slices of cucumber on the whole one. Then, lay the circle with the hole on top.
7. Cut another two circles of bread and cut a hole in one of them. Spread butter and jam on the whole one. Press the circles together.

— Crib pies —

You will need:

- 340g shortcrust pastry
- 1 jar mincemeat
- A little beaten egg or milk
- Caster sugar for dusting

Method

1. Roll out the pastry and cut into rectangles about 12cm by 8cm. Put half the rectangles to one side.
2. Place a teaspoon of mincemeat in the middle of each of the remaining rectangles.
3. Brush a little milk or egg around the edges of each filled rectangle and make lids from the rectangles you set aside. Crimp the edges to seal into a 'crib' shape.
4. Cut circles from the pastry leftovers to make the baby's head. Mark eyes and a mouth and tuck the head beneath a pastry 'blanket' on top of each crib.
5. Bake at 220C for 20 minutes or until the pies look golden.
6. Cool on a wire tray and dust with caster sugar.

— Spiced ruby punch —

You will need:

- 1 litre cranberry juice
- 2.5 litres ginger ale or lemonade
- Juice of a lemon
- 6 cinnamon sticks
- A few whole allspice
- A few cloves
- 2 apples, thinly sliced
- 1 lemon, thinly sliced

Method

1. Pour the cranberry juice, lemon juice and ginger ale into a large saucepan.

2. Add the cinnamon sticks and spices. Bring to the boil and simmer for 20 minutes.
3. Strain off the cinnamon and spices and carefully pour the liquid into a jug.
4. Add the apple and lemon slices and serve warm. (The punch can be served cold if preferred.)

Creative ideas for the countdown to Christmas

Many children today will have Advent calendars, often with a secular picture on the front and with chocolates behind the doors. Although these are far removed from the original idea of Advent calendars, they do at least mean that the children are aware of the weeks and days leading up to Christmas.

The season of Advent reminds us to think about when Jesus will come again. We must prepare for this day—but we do not know when it will be. The times of preparation in church, Advent and Lent, both use purple as their liturgical colour. Purple was the colour of kings and the colour of mourning; it links the kingship of Jesus with his humanity, birth and death.

❄ ✳ ❄

— Advent candles —

You will need:

Five candles: three purple, one pink (or blue) and one white; candle holders; matches or candle lighter

Advent means 'coming', so it is a time of looking forward to the coming of Jesus and preparing our hearts for such a special event. We celebrate with five candles. Each has a meaning, which is explained below. One candle is lit on each of the four Sundays leading up to Christmas, with the last one being lit on Christmas Day.

There are instructions on page 88 for making an Advent wreath for the candles. You may wish to write the explanation for each candle on a sheet of card and display it as a reminder of the meaning as each candle is lit.

First candle (purple)

We light this candle on the first Sunday in Advent. It represents the Patriarchs, who are the founding fathers of the Old Testament: Abraham, Isaac and Jacob. These men had faith in one God, unlike the people around them who worshipped lots of different gods. God used their faith to form them into a 'covenant people'.

Second candle (purple)

We light this candle on the second Sunday in Advent. It represents the prophets of the Old Testament—for example, Isaiah, Jeremiah and Micah. They told about the coming of Jesus and urged people to prepare themselves for this event.

Third candle (pink)

We light this candle on the third Sunday in Advent. It reminds us of Mary, who was visited by the angel Gabriel and was obedient to God. She gave birth to Jesus and reminds us all to act to bring about God's kingdom on earth. The colour marks the change from Old to New Testament. In some churches, a blue candle is used on this day because blue is the traditional colour used for Mary.

Fourth candle (purple)

We light this candle on the fourth Sunday in Advent. It represents John the Baptist, the last of the prophets. John told people about Jesus and recognised that Jesus was the Son of God. John also tells us that we need to prepare ourselves to meet Jesus.

Fifth candle (white)

We light this candle on Christmas Day because it represents Jesus as the light for the world, breaking in on our darkness. The change of colour helps us to remember that our lives are different when Jesus shines his light into our hearts. White is the colour that the church uses for celebrations such as the great festivals of Christmas and Easter.

❄ ✱ ❄

— Advent chain —

You will need:

Advent chain sheets, downloaded from **www.barnabasinchurches.org.uk/ pdfs/creativeideas.pdf**; stick glue

The wording for each chain is given on pages 49–50 for reference, but the downloadable file will give you the option to print out the chains as A4 sheets.

Advent chains can be easily made by children of all ages and hung in the home as an alternative to an Advent calendar.

- Print out the sheets and cut into strips. Assemble the chain by using the strips as links. Secure each link with a dab of stick glue.
- Hang the chain up. Remove one link for each day of December and complete the activity on the link. Adjust the hanging position as the chain shortens each day.
- If you wish, you can use different coloured paper for weekdays and Sundays. You may also wish to decorate the plain side of the links with coloured pens or crayons.

Creative ideas for the countdown to Christmas

1. Say a prayer for all those who are lonely	

2. Offer to set the table for dinner	

3. Ask permission to make cupcakes for the family	

4. Be nice to someone you don't like very much	

5. Offer to say grace at a meal time	

6. Read about St Nicholas, whose feast day is today	

7. Say a prayer for all the people who are in hospital	

8. Look at the night sky and see if you can recognise any star constellations	

9. Make a Christmas card for someone	

10. Send the Christmas card you made yesterday	

11. Make a Christmas tree ornament from old cards	

12. Hug everyone in your family today	

13. Say a prayer for all the world's homeless people

14. Write 'I love you' notes to members of your family and hide them under their pillows

15. Find a story about Christmas in another country

16. Offer to do the dusting

17. Practise singing Christmas carols

18. Clean your bedroom without being asked

19. Say a prayer for all the world's hungry people

20. Offer to help with wrapping presents

21. Suggest making Christmas biscuits as a family

22. Make sure your room is tidy

23. Read Luke 2:1–20 with your family

24. Set up your crib scene

❄ ✶ ❄

— Advent alphabet —

You will need:

A large square of medium-weight card; ruler and pencil for marking the squares; coloured pens or crayons; a length of ribbon; sticky tape

You might like to make an alphabet chart of symbols connected to the Advent season, adding one symbol every day during Advent or December. Ideas for each day are given below.

Make the chart by marking the squares on a piece of medium-weight card. Decorate the chart with pens or crayons to give a Christmassy feel and think about what symbol you would use for each of the alphabet items. Affix a length of ribbon to the top of the chart with sticky tape. Hang the chart somewhere where it can be easily removed to fill in the symbols each day.

If you wish, you could also find the story for each of the symbols in the Bible and talk about that part of the Christmas story.

1. A is for… (angel Gabriel)

2. B is for… (Bethlehem)

3. C is for… (census)

4. D is for… (donkey)

5. E is for… (Elizabeth)

6. F is for… (flocks)

7. G is for… (God with us)

8. H is for… (Herod)

9. I is for… (inn)

10. J is for… (Joseph)

11. K is for… (king of the Jews)

12. L is for… (light)

13. M is for… (Mary)

14. N is for… (night)

15. O is for… (obey)

16. P is for… (prophets)

17. Q is for… (quest)

18. R is for… (rushing)

19. S is for… (shepherds)

20. T is for… (treasure)

21. U is for… (under a star)

22. V is for… (visitors)

23. W is for… (wise men's gifts)

24. XYZ is for… (baby in the manger; the love that has no end)

Creative ideas for the countdown to Christmas

A is for…	B is for…	C is for…	D is for…	E is for…	F is for…
G is for…	H is for…	I is for…	J is for…	K is for…	L is for…
M is for…	N is for…	O is for…	P is for…	Q is for…	R is for…
S is for…	T is for…	U is for…	V is for…	W is for…	XYZ is for…

❄ ✱ ❄

— Advent gifts —

You will need:

A small tree in a pot (twigs in soil would do); 24 small wrapped sweets, or sweets wrapped in foil to keep them fresh; 24 pipe cleaners; 24 square pieces of coloured paper (about 10cm square)

This activity is a three-dimensional alternative to a chocolate Advent calendar, with the added advantage that the tree itself becomes a decorated feature at the end of Advent. If the activity is to be shared between several children, you can either increase the number of sweets or arrange for the children to take turns to unwrap the sweets day by day.

Wrap each sweet in the middle of a piece of paper and fold the corners in. Bend a pipe cleaner around each parcel to make it look like a present. Place the gifts in a bowl or box by the tree.

Each day during December, take a gift and unwrap it carefully. Smooth out the paper and zigzag-fold it like a fan. Wrap the pipe cleaner around the middle of the paper and fan out the ends to make the paper resemble a bow. Use the ends of the pipe cleaner to tie the bow on to the tree.

On Christmas Day, the gifts will have gone and the tree will be decorated.

❄ ✱ ❄

— Advent house —

You will need:

Two large sheets of paper or thin card; paper; colouring materials; decorations; scissors; glue

This house is a weekly Advent calendar.

Attach the two sheets of paper or card together and draw a large house on the top sheet. Cut round the outline through both sheets, to make two identical houses.

On one house shape, draw in the roof, four large windows and a door. Write the dates of the four Sundays in Advent, one on each window. Colour and decorate the house. When it is dry, carefully cut around three sides of each window and the door, then cut the door so that it has a top and bottom half.

Encourage the children to make pictures to go behind each window and each half of the door. Stick the decorated house on top of the plain house shape, remembering first to stick the pictures on to the bottom sheet, behind the windows and doors. On the inside of the window and door flaps, write a suitable Bible reference or verse, so that the verse can be seen when the flaps are opened.

Each Sunday during Advent, open one of the windows together and read the verse. Open the top half of the door on Christmas Eve and the lower half on Christmas Day.

You may like to say the following prayer together.

Father God, as we prepare for the birth of Jesus, we ask that you will be with us and bless us. Amen

— Advent village —

You will need:

A large sheet of thick card; thin card; paper; paint and glitter; scissors and glue; template for houses; a large bowl of sweets or small gifts

This Advent calendar takes a lot of work and time, but is well worth making.

In advance, you will need to make a base board for your Advent village. On the large piece of thick card, draw a plan of the roads and paint it to look like a map of a village. Use glitter to highlight certain areas. You may like to include snow. Make trees and plants to give the base a three-dimensional effect.

Each day during Advent, another house is added to the scene, so you will need 24 houses if you start on 1 December, or more if you start on Advent Sunday. Make sure the date is written somewhere on each house.

Every day, someone adds a house to the village and, in exchange, takes a sweet or small gift.

❄ ✱ ❄

— Stocking countdown —

You will need:

24 small Christmas stockings or small socks; 24 sticky labels; 24 small pegs; a length of thin ribbon or strong yarn; 24 small gifts or wrapped sweets; 24 pieces of paper with a nice patterned border and enough room to write or draw on; small bowl or box; pen or pencil

Stick the numbers 1 to 24 on each stocking and put a small gift or wrapped sweet in each one.

Hang the length of ribbon or yarn in a convenient place and attach the 24 stockings to it with the pegs. Put the 24 pieces of paper in a bowl or box, along with a pen or pencil.

Starting on 1 December, every day (taking turns day by day) someone takes the gift from the stocking. In exchange, they must write a prayer or message or draw a picture on one of the pieces of paper and put it in the empty stocking.

After Christmas you could gather together and read all the prayers and messages.

❄ ✶ ❄

— Advent purses —

You will need:

Enough white felt to make 24 purses; purse template (see page 119); red or green sewing thread and needles; 24 buttons (the same colour as the sewing thread); a length of festive ribbon, long enough to thread each purse on to; small presents or wrapped sweets; thin card; hole punch; festive thread; colouring pens; scissors

In the Anglican calendar, the countdown to Advent starts four weeks before Advent Sunday. This time can be used to make an Advent calendar, in preparation for starting the countdown proper in December.

Cut out 24 purses using the template. Fold up at the bottom dotted line and sew on a button. Stitch around the edge (perhaps using blanket stitch). Embroider the numbers 1 to 24 on the flaps of the purses. Attach a length of thread (about 10cm) to the centre of the flap to wind around the button. Put a small gift in each purse and thread each purse on to the ribbon, winding the length of thread around the button on each purse. Hang the garland.

Cut 24 circles of thin card (about 3cm in diameter) and decorate them with Christmassy designs. Punch a hole in the top of each circle and thread with festive thread to make a hanging loop.

Each day during December, whoever takes the gift from the purse recloses the purse and hangs one of the circle decorations from the button to show that the gift has been taken.

＊

Creative ideas for Advent and Christmas prayers

Simple items can provide an effective focus for praying with children and are ideal for many situations at church and in the home. In the home, the objects used for the ideas in this section could be kept in a special place so that they are to hand when moments for praying together present themselves. They are special times to share.

Basic equipment includes colouring materials, card, scissors, ribbon, glitter, glue, pens and pencils.

❄ ✱ ❄

— Christmas stars —

Stars of all sizes can be cut from medium-weight card (see page 120 for basic templates for small and large stars). You will also need to provide craft items, such as colouring materials, scissors, glue, ribbon, a hole punch, pencils and pens, and sticky tack for mounting the stars if needed.

Older children will be able to cut out their own stars from a template provided, whereas younger children will need to have the stars pre-cut for them.

Cut out enough stars for everyone to have one, or make some star templates and let every member of the group make their own star.

Invite everyone to write one-line prayers on the stars, thanking God for the gift of his own Son on that first Christmas Day. Decorate the edges of the prayer stars with glitter, then punch a hole in the top of each one and attach a piece of ribbon so that they can be hung on the Christmas tree.

❄ ★ ❄

— Stars in the sky —

Cut out enough stars for everyone to have one, or make some star templates and let every member of the group make their own star. Invite everyone to write a prayer on their star. They can then be decorated as desired and stuck on to a large piece of card acting as a 'sky' background. Alternatively, punch a hole in the top of each star, attach a piece of ribbon and hang them on the background.

❄ ★ ❄

— Large stars —

Cut out enough large stars for everyone to have one, or make some star templates and let every member of the group make their own star. Choose from the ideas below, and then decorate the stars as desired.

- Ask younger children to write a simple five-word prayer on the points of the star.
- Larger stars could be used by older children to think of five 'prayer pointers' throughout Advent or for the four Sundays of Advent and Christmas Day.
- Some might like to write prayers on the stars and give them to members of the congregation as a present.
- Prayer stars from the whole group could be mounted on a wall behind a crib or nativity scene.
- A very large star cut-out could be mounted on a plain circular sheet of card. The five points of the star could become the doors of a five-week Advent calendar. The children could draw pictures behind each point or door as a focus for prayer. The doors can then be opened out on the appropriate day.

❄ ✶ ❄

— Prayer candles —

You will need:

A candle and card circle for everyone. The card circle needs to be approximately 10cm in diameter. Cut four or five 1.5cm slits out from the centre of the card circle (see diagram below) to hold the candle in place.

Invite the congregation to write or draw on their circle things they want to pray for. You might need to suggest events, or someone who is ill, and so on. Invite everyone to write something they want to ask God about for themselves. Then insert the candle in its card circle holder. The candles can be lit and a general prayer said.

Prayer candles can be used in Sunday and midweek groups, or perhaps used regularly during prayer times at home.

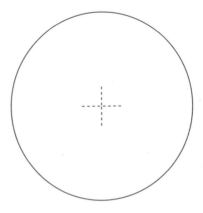

— Holly wreath —

Give out paper holly leaves (see template on page 121) and invite people to write short prayers on them. Young children can draw something about Christmas on theirs. Stick all the prayers on to a circle of card and add a few red paper berries. Attach a ribbon and hang the prayer wreath on a door.

❄ ✱ ❄

— Gift of praise —

Make a gift of praise for God. Giftwrap a small cardboard box and tie a bright ribbon around it, or paste a large square of giftwrap on to backing paper and add ribbons so that it looks like a present. Then, give out small pieces of paper or sticky labels and ask the members of the group each to draw or write something that they want to thank God for. Play some quiet music while people come up one at a time to paste or stick their prayers on to the box.

Write out the following Bible verse on a piece of card and it display beside the box.

We thank you, our God, and praise you.
1 CHRONICLES 29:13

❄ ✱ ❄

— Snowflakes —

Give each person a circle of paper and show them how to fold and cut it to make a snowflake. (If you don't have enough scissors for everyone, you might like to try tearing the paper instead.) When everyone has cut their own snowflake and unfolded it to reveal the shape, compare the different patterns. You should find that no two snowflakes are identical.

Microscopes reveal that snowflakes are made up of tiny six-sided ice crystals, and no two crystals are exactly the same. No two people are identical, either. Each person is unique; even twins are really quite different from one another.

As a group, compose a prayer praising God that each person is special and unique, and thanking him that he knows each of us inside out. He even knows how many hairs we have on our heads. Write out the prayer and stick it on to a sheet of black or dark blue paper, with all the snowflakes displayed around the edge.

❋ ✷ ❋

— Balloon prayers —

Have ready a number of inflated balloons and a selection of permanent marker pens. Invite everyone to suggest one-line 'thank you' prayers and write two or three prayers on each balloon. Hang the balloons in clusters around your church or meeting room—perhaps as part of a special celebration service. Balloon prayers can also be made in the home and hung alongside the Christmas decorations.

❋ ✷ ❋

— Pop the balloon —

Have ready a number of inflated balloons and a selection of permanent marker pens. Invite everyone to name some of the reasons we might need to say 'sorry' to God. Write them on the balloons.

Then have a few moments of prayer, asking God's forgiveness for all the things we do wrong, including the suggestions written on the balloons. Finally, pop the balloons and explain that when we say sorry to God, he not only forgives us but he also forgets the wrong things we have done and gives us the chance to make a fresh start.

❈ ✹ ❈

— Prayer paper chain —

Give everyone a strip of coloured paper and encourage them to write a one-line 'thank you' prayer. Fasten all the strips together to make a festive paper chain that you can hang across the room. If you have a small group, you might want to give each person two or three strips of paper or add to the chain week by week.

The prayer paper chain is particularly effective on special occasions, such as Christmas and church anniversaries, when a long chain can be made during an all-age service.

❈ ✹ ❈

— A host of angels —

You will need:

Dark backing paper; angel template (see page 122); glue; pens; glitter; sticky stars

Tell the story of how the angels appeared to the shepherds in the field one dark night (Luke 2:8–20). With younger children, you might like to use a version from a children's Bible such as *The Barnabas Children's Bible* (Barnabas, 2007).

Give everyone a copy of the angel template and ask them to write their own short prayer on the angel's robe, thanking God for the gift of his Son at Christmas. Anyone who is unsure what to write might consider copying the angels' words from Luke 2:14.

'Praise God in heaven! Peace on earth to everyone who pleases God.'
LUKE 2:14

Young children could colour in their angel shape in bright colours. Play some Christmas music while everyone glues their angel on to the backing paper, so that the finished collage looks like a host of angels. As a finishing touch, add a sprinkling of glitter and sticky stars to the backing paper.

❄ ✶ ❄

— Gift-shaped prayers —

You will need:

A large outline of a Christmas tree, sized up on to card from the template on page 123; tinsel; squares and rectangles of coloured paper or large sticky labels

Take a moment to think about those people for whom Christmas will not be happy this year. They could include people who have been recently bereaved, those in war-torn countries, those who are ill, those who have lost their jobs recently and so on. All these needy people deserve a special Christmas present and, even though we may not know many of these people personally, we can still give them the gift of our prayers.

Give out the squares and rectangles of paper and invite everyone to write their own prayers for those in need this Christmas. Stick all the prayer-presents on to the outline of the Christmas tree. Write the words from the Bible verse below on a piece of card and stick it on to the bottom of the tree.

Never stop praying, especially for others.
EPHESIANS 6:18

Decorate the tree with tinsel and offer all the gifts to God in a concluding prayer.

Creative uses for Christmas cards

It is always worth saving Christmas cards from the previous year, as there are many ways that they can be recycled. The ideas in this section can be used in Sunday and midweek groups, as well as in the home. For group activities, if you don't have enough cards from your own stores, you may find that a request to the wider congregation will supply your needs.

❅ ✱ ❅

— Christmas boxes —

You will need:

Copies of the Christmas box template on page 124 (one per person); Christmas cards; scissors; glue; glittery thread; small gifts or wrapped sweets

Make little Christmas boxes which can be used as gift boxes on the Christmas table or hung on the Christmas tree. You can also use them as containers for homemade sweets.

Either copy the template on to the back of a Christmas card picture or stick it on the back (you may need to adjust the size to fit your chosen card). Stick the tabs down and don't forget to pop a small gift inside before securing the lid.

Attach a length of glittery thread to one corner of the box if you're going to use it as a tree decoration.

❄ ✦ ❄

— Gift tags —

Making gift tags is a traditional use for old Christmas cards but it never fails to amuse children and adults alike.

You will need:

Christmas cards; pinking shears or scissors with a serrated cutting edge; hole punch; ribbon

Use the pinking shears or serrated scissors to cut out attractive pictures from your cards. Use a hole punch to make a hole in one corner and thread gift ribbon through.

❄ ✦ ❄

— Gift bags —

Save good-quality brown (or any colour) paper bags, preferably without any labels on them. Cut an attractive picture out of a Christmas card and stick it to the front of the bag. Add a ribbon bow above the picture and wrap a gift in tissue paper before putting it in the bag.

Brown paper bags and tartan ribbon look very attractive.

❄ ✦ ❄

— Desktop wallpaper —

Make some Christmassy wallpaper for your computer by scanning your favourite cards into the computer and then making them into a montage using a photo program or Publisher program. Use the design as Christmas wallpaper or a screensaver at Christmas. Children enjoy doing this and it can make a good memento of Christmas if done every year.

❄ ✳ ❄

— Christmas confetti —

Use a plain hole punch and a Christmas-shape hole punch (a snowflake or Christmas tree is ideal) and punch shapes from Christmas cards. Gold and silver areas of card look very effective, especially mixed in with red and green. This activity keeps children occupied for hours.

❄ ✳ ❄

— Toddler's lacing card —

Choose a suitable card and laminate it. Punch holes around the edge using a hole punch and add a brightly coloured shoelace. Lacing cards are great for little fingers and suitable for children aged 2–4.

❄ ✳ ❄

— Telling the Christmas story —

Sort the cards into those with pictures that tell the Christmas story we hear in the Bible, and those with pictures that are traditionally associated with Christmas but are not part of the Bible story.

The cards can be used to tell the story chronologically. When you are telling the story, talk about some of the symbols on the cards and what they mean—for example, a dove, light, a star and so on.

Some cards can be laminated and turned into simple jigsaw puzzles, which could be used with younger children while telling the story shown on the card.

Alternatively, sort the cards to tell the Christmas story as it is given in Matthew's Gospel and in Luke's Gospel. Print out the stories from the two Gospels. The stories will include the following events.

- The angel visits Mary (Luke 1:26–38)
- Mary visits Elizabeth, and Mary's song of praise (Luke 1:39–56)
- The birth of Jesus (Luke 2:1–7)
- The shepherds visit Bethlehem (Luke 2:8–20)
- Simeon and Anna praise the Lord (Luke 1:22–38)
- Visitors from the east (Matthew 2:1–12)
- The escape to Egypt (Matthew 2:13–15)

Place the Bible verses alongside each other and put the cards by the appropriate verses. Ask the children why they think Matthew and Luke wrote different parts of the Christmas story.

Select the cards that show an artist's interpretation of the Christmas story. Ask the children why they think the artist painted the picture in the way they did.

Look at cards that show the Christmas story from the perspective of a different culture. Ask the children what this helps us to understand about the Christmas story.

— Christmas bingo —

You will need:

Sets of identical Christmas cards (or wrapping paper with repeated patterns) from which you can cut out several copies of the same pictures; six pieces of thin card (A5 size), divided into six (or more) squares or rectangles; glue; counters or squares of card to cover the pictures when playing

Cut out the pictures from the cards or wrapping paper and stick them on to the thin cards to make bingo playing cards. Use some of the same pictures on each bingo card, but make sure the finished cards are not identical.

To play the game, call out a Christmas-related picture and, if anyone has that picture on their game card, they cover it up with a counter.

The first person to cover all their pictures shouts, 'Don't be afraid!' These are the words that many of the angels in the Christmas story used when they visited people with news about Jesus.

*

Creative ideas for Christmas decorations

— Lanterns —

You will need:

Rectangles of brightly coloured paper (one per person); scissors; glue; sheets of gold paper, kitchen foil or cellophane

Fold a rectangle of brightly coloured paper in half widthways and make cuts from the folded edge to within 2cm of the open edge. Unfold the paper carefully and bend it into a circle, pressing the two ends together towards the centre. Glue at the top and bottom.

Take some paper the same width but not quite so deep and make a roll to fit inside the lantern like a tube. (This looks very effective if you use gold paper, kitchen foil or cellophane.) Glue a strip of paper to the outside as a handle.

❄ ✳ ❄

— Hand and footprint angels —

You will need:

A sheet of heavyweight paper, craft foam or poster board; a sheet of white paper; permanent markers; scissors; colouring material; painting materials (optional); glue; a photo of each child (optional); pipe cleaners or ribbon; shiny giftwrap or tinfoil

This Christmas angel has a footprint body and two handprint wings. Use a heavyweight paper, craft foam or poster board for a longer-lasting version.

Ask a child to stand on the paper, poster board or craft foam with his or her feet together. Draw round the feet to form the angel's body and dress. Next, ask the child to press both hands flat on to the white paper. Draw round both hands. Alternatively, use yellow paint and make a paint handprint. These shapes will form the wings. They look better if the fingers are not spread too far apart. Decorate the dress and wings as desired.

Cut out a circle to make the angel's head (or use a photo of the child). Assemble the angel by folding the body in half to form a back and a front and gluing in place. (Alternatively, you can leave the feet unfolded.) Glue the head to the heel end of the body shape and the wings to the body.

Add a halo if desired. The halo can be formed by using a pipe cleaner or ribbon shaped as a halo, or by cutting out a many-pointed star shape from card. Alternatively, you could just use a simple card circle (depending on how energetic you are feeling). Shiny giftwrap or tinfoil makes an effective alternative to card. Paste the halo behind the head, so that the head is totally surrounded.

Write the following poem either on the back of the dress or on a separate tag, using appropriate wording depending whether the child is a boy or a girl.

This little angel is special, you see
Because s/he is a part of me.
Her/his wings are my hands,
Her/his body my feet,
And on the tree s/he'll look very sweet.

You can also add the child's name and the year and a ribbon if you wish to hang the angel on the Christmas tree.

— Circle stars —

You will need:

A circle of card with the middle cut out (like a polo mint) and five holes punched around the ring at equal intervals (see template on page 125); Christmassy yarn; sewing needle with a large eye; sticky tape

Cut about 2m of yarn. Thread the yarn up through Hole 1, leave about 30cm dangling and tape the yarn on the wrong side behind this hole so that it will not slip. Now take the yarn down through Hole 2 and up through Hole 3, and then down through Hole 4 and up through Hole 5.

Now take the yarn down through Hole 1, up through Hole 2, down through Hole 3, up through Hole 4 and down through Hole 5. Finally, take the yarn up through Hole 1.

Tie this last piece of thread to the dangly bit from the beginning of the process, and the star is ready to hang.

❄ ✳ ❄

— Cone tree —

You will need:

Thin card; felt-tipped pens or paints; glitter and decorations; glue; a short cardboard tube, such as the inside of a roll of kitchen paper

To make tall, thin trees, draw a circle on thin card approximately 25cm in diameter, cut it out and cut the circle into four quarters. Roll one quarter into a cone shape with the edges slightly overlapping and stick down.

For the trunk, either colour a short cardboard tube brown or roll a strip of thin card approximately 4cm by 10cm into a tube and stick the edges down. Secure the trunk to the cone with plenty of glue.

To make shorter, fatter trees, draw a circle on thin card about 25cm in diameter, cut it out and cut the circle into two halves. Roll one half into a cone shape with the edges slightly overlapping and stick down. For the trunk, either colour a short cardboard tube brown or roll a strip of thin card approximately 8cm by 15cm into a tube and stick the edges down. Secure the trunk to the cone with plenty of glue.

The thin card can be coloured before folding into a cone, and decorations can be added after the tree has been stuck together.

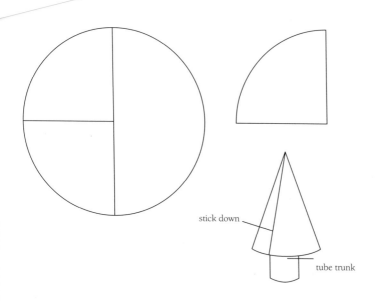

stick down

tube trunk

※ ✱ ※

— A chime of bells —

You will need:

Egg cartons; silver or gold spray paint; foil, beads or small Christmas baubles for clappers; narrow ribbon and decorative yarn

Cut out the sections from the egg cartons and spray them silver or gold. Use plenty of newspaper to protect surfaces. Pierce a hole in the middle of each section and thread them with decorative yarn. Tie on a clapper made from a piece of foil, a bead or a small bauble.

Hang the bells together in clusters of three or four on different lengths of yarn. Knot them together and tie with a bow of ribbon.

Yoghurt pots or drinking cups can be used to make bigger bells.

❄ ✷ ❄

— Egg box baubles —

You will need:

Egg cartons; spray or poster paint; glitter, sequins, braid and beads;
narrow ribbon or decorative yarn; PVA glue

Cut two sections from an egg carton for each bauble. Make a hole
in the centre of one of the sections and insert a thread from which
to hang the finished bauble. Thread a bead or tassel through the
bottom end of the piece of thread to secure it, and fasten the top
end of the thread so that the bauble can be hung. Place the shapes
with the wide edges together. Stick the sections together, using
plenty of glue.

Paint or spray the finished baubles and decorate them with
glitter, sequins and braid.

Larger baubles can be made by gluing two foil cake cases or
drinking cups together.

A string of baubles can be made by threading individual baubles
together.

❄ ✷ ❄

— Dough decorations —

You will need:

A cup of salt; a cup of flour; water and cooking oil; rolling pin; knitting
needle; paints and varnish; glue; festive yarn or ribbon

Mix the salt and flour together and stir in enough water to make
a stiff paste. Adding a little cooking oil will make the dough more
manageable.

Use the dough to make tree decorations. A ball could be used to make a Christmas pudding or Christmas bauble. Put some flour on a rolling pin and a clean surface and roll out the dough. Cut shapes from the dough and pierce a hole in the top of each decoration with a knitting needle.

Place the decorations on a baking tray and bake in a cool oven until the dough has set. When the decorations have cooled, paint, varnish and decorate them, and thread yarn or ribbon through the hole to hang them.

❄ ✲ ❄

— Gingerbread shapes —

You will need:

A thin slab of ready-made gingerbread; biscuit cutters; knife; knitting needle; thin ribbon or thick yarn; icing sugar; bowl

Cut out shapes using the biscuit cutters. Stars, trees and hearts are all seasonal. Push a knitting needle through the top of each shape and thread the ribbon or yarn through to make a hanging loop. Mix up the icing sugar with some water in a bowl and use it to decorate the shapes.

❄ ✲ ❄

— Pomanders —

You will need:

An orange for each pomander; cocktail sticks; 50g whole cloves; 25g powdered orris root; 25g ground cinnamon; greaseproof paper; 1 metre of ribbon

Stick as many cloves as possible into the orange, using a cocktail stick to make small holes first. Arrange the cloves in a pattern. Once the cloves are inserted, rub the orange with a mixture of equal parts of cinnamon and orris root. Wrap the pomander in greaseproof paper and leave for about a month. Finally, remove the pomander from the paper and wrap the ribbon firmly around the preserved orange. Make a decorative hanging loop.

Pomanders can be made without rubbing the cinnamon and orris root mixture on to them and leaving them to dry, but they do not last anywhere near as long.

❄ ✳ ❄

— Expanding people —

You will need:

Paper; scraps of decorative paper; glue; scissors; thread

Take a rectangle of paper and fold it in half. Cut slits from each edge alternately, making sure you don't cut straight across. Open the paper out carefully, as this makes the body. Add heads and faces at the top and feet at the bottom. Arms can be stuck to the sides.

Have fun experimenting to make Christmas characters and figures of different sizes by using different sized rectangles of paper. Use the thread to suspend the characters by their heads.

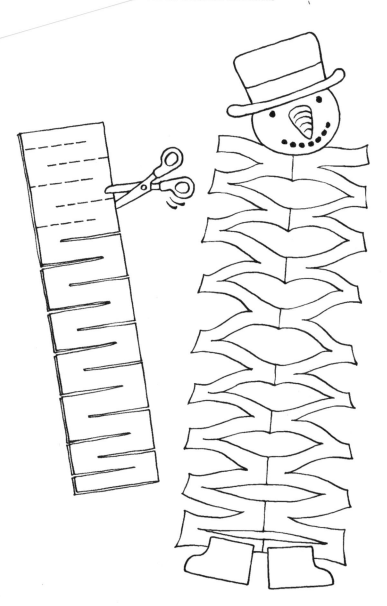

❆ ✳ ❆

— Glittery garlands —

You will need:

Packet of crêpe paper; glitter; PVA glue; scissors; newspaper

Take the crêpe paper out of its packet and, without unrolling it, cut a strip off the end, about 5cm wide. **NB:** The crinkles on the crêpe paper will be running down, not along, the strip.

Now unroll the strip you have cut off, and lay it on a piece of newspaper. Brush a line of PVA glue along the middle of the strip and sprinkle glitter on it. Leave to dry, then turn the strip over and decorate the other side in the same way.

When the glue is almost dry, gently wrap the strip of paper around and around your hand and then carefully slide it off. Keeping the paper folded, make repeated snips along both edges, cutting as far as the band of glitter. Be careful not to cut through the band. Unfold the crêpe paper and twist it to make a garland. Leave it for about three hours before hanging it up.

Glue two different coloured pieces of crêpe paper together, before twisting, to make a double-sided garland.

Garlands can be made as long as you like by gluing several together, end to end.

❆ ✳ ❆

— Paper garlands —

You will need:

Gift ribbon; wrapping paper or coloured paper; scissors; glue; star stickers and sequins

Cut a very long piece of the gift ribbon. Fold the wrapping paper or coloured paper in half and cut circles (or other shapes) through both layers so that you have matching pairs of circles. Spread glue on one of the circles and lay the ribbon on top. Then, press the other circle on top, matching the edges.

Repeat this process, using lots of circles, and gluing them along the ribbon with small spaces left in between the circles. In some places, press the ribbon on to a star sticker, then add another sticker on top, matching the edges. When you have filled the ribbon with shapes, decorate some of the plain circles by gluing on little sequins.

These garlands look effective hanging vertically with pieces of ribbon in between them.

❄ ✲ ❄

— Festive spice tree —

You will need:

Floral oasis pyramid and a base to stand it on; florist's tape; sprigs of greenery (fir or yew); sprigs of holly; fine wire; ribbon or tinsel bows; cinnamon sticks; vanilla pods, citrus peel, nutmegs and cloves; satsumas or tangerines

Soak the piece of floral oasis in water and tape it securely on to the base. Stick sprigs of greenery and holly into the oasis to make a tree shape. Wire together the cinnamon sticks, vanilla pods, citrus peel and other spices. Push these 'spice kebabs' into the foliage.

Decorate with ribbon or tinsel bows, and arrange satsumas around the finished spice tree. You now have a lovely, spicy-smelling decoration.

✷

Creative ideas for party games

— Nativity pass-the-parcel —

You will need:

A prize (perhaps a small book of the Christmas story); a set of small nativity figures; a small tree or crib scene

This is a popular and simple game to play. A parcel is passed around a circle while music is played and, when the music stops, whoever is holding the parcel undoes one layer of wrapping. The music then restarts and the parcel is passed around again until the last layer of wrapping reveals the main prize.

Prepare the parcel by wrapping up the prize. Between each of the layers place a small nativity figure. You will need to put the three wise men in between the first three layers, then the shepherds and any sheep (one in each layer), the angels and then baby Jesus, followed by any animals. Joseph goes in before Mary.

As the game proceeds and each layer reveals a figure, tell the Christmas story and place the figure on the tree or in the crib scene. This will make the game last longer.

Older children might like to tell the part of the story they have unwrapped themselves.

✳ ✶ ✳

— Pass-the-parcel without a CD player —

You will need:

A prepared parcel; the words of the song printed below

If you don't have access to recorded music, this simple song can be sung to the tune of 'London's burning'.

Pass the parcel, pass the parcel,
Don't drop it! Don't drop it!
Keep it moving, keep it moving,
Now pass it … times more.

When the children sing 'Now pass it … times more' the leader adds a number—for example, 'Now pass it seven times more'. The parcel is then passed on another seven times. A bit of quick calculation will ensure that every child has a turn at unwrapping the parcel.

✳ ✶ ✳

— Nativity consequences —

You will need:

A piece of plain paper for each person playing; a pencil or pen

This is a variation on the traditional game of consequences, but with no words. The aim is to draw a character from the Christmas story, such as a shepherd or an angel or Mary, one stage at a time.

Give everyone a piece of paper and a pencil and ask them to draw a shepherd's hat. When this has been done, ask them to fold over the paper so that the hat can't be seen and pass it to the person on their left.

The next person draws the shepherd's head and neck, folds the paper over again and passes it to the person on their left.

The next person draws the shepherd's body (as far as the waist) and arms.

The next person draws the shepherd's lower body and legs, but no feet.

The next person draws the shepherd's feet and chooses a name for the shepherd.

The final person gets to undo the paper and reveal the picture.

❊ ✴ ❊

— Guess the carol —

You will need:

The titles of a selection of Christmas carols written on slips of paper, folded and placed in a bowl or similar container; paper, pens and pencils for each team; a clock or watch with a second hand

Divide the group into two (or more) teams and give each team some paper and pens and pencils. Someone in each team picks a piece of paper from the bowl and they then have 30 seconds to draw the carol. When the time is up, the teams try to guess each other's carol.

❊ ✴ ❊

— Mary and Joseph are going to Bethlehem —

Ask everyone to sit in a circle on chairs or on the floor.

The first person says, 'Mary and Joseph are going to Bethlehem and they are taking a donkey.' The next person says, 'Mary and

Joseph are going to Bethlehem and they are taking a blanket and a donkey.' The next person says, 'Mary and Joseph are going to Bethlehem and they are taking a ...' adding an object and repeating 'a blanket and a donkey'. The game continues in the same way.

Everyone takes it in turn to speak until someone forgets the objects or the order of the objects. That person then drops out and does not take part in the game any more. The game continues until there is an overall winner, or finishes when nobody can remember all of the objects in the right order.

❄ ✭ ❄

— Angel musical chairs —

You will need:

Enough chairs for all the children (decorate one chair with angel wings or some tinsel to represent an angel's halo); music

Set up a circle or line of chairs to play musical chairs. Play the game as normal, except that when the music stops, the child sitting on the angel chair will be out. Remove one chair each time and the game continues. The last child left standing will be the winner.

❄ ✭ ❄

— Pin the halo on the angel —

You will need:

A large picture of an angel without a halo; enough halos for each child to have one (made of card or thick paper); sticky tack; a blindfold

Each child takes it in turns to be blindfolded and tries to stick the halo above the angel's head.

❄ ✦ ❄

— Angel, angel, where's your halo? —

You will need:

A pair of angel wings; an angel's halo (made out of tinsel)

One child is chosen to be the angel and wears the angel wings. The remaining children sit in a circle with the 'angel' in the middle. The children pass the halo around behind their backs. When the leader says, 'Angel, angel, where's your halo?' they stop passing the halo and the angel has to guess who has the halo behind their back. If the angel guesses correctly, they swap places and the game continues. If the angel does not guess who has the halo, the angel has another turn.

❄ ✦ ❄

— Tree ornament relay —

You will need:

A large paper Christmas tree for each team, fixed to the wall; a paper tree decoration with a piece of sticky tack on the back for each child

Divide the children into equal teams. One at a time, the team members run to their tree and stick their decoration on the tree. The first team to stick all their decorations on their tree is the winner.

You can extend the game by having two or three tree decorations for each child, or by using a real tree and decorations. Real decorations will need to have easy-to-use hangers.

❊ ✳ ❊

— Quick-draw Christmas story —

You will need:

A large piece of paper for each team; a pencil or pen for each child

The aim of this game is for each team to draw a picture of the Christmas story. Divide the children into teams. Give each team a large sheet of paper and a pencil for each child. Explain that on the word 'Go!' the first person in the team must draw something from the scene at Jesus' birth. On the word 'Change!' the next person takes over as artist and draws something else.

The game can continue for as long as you like, but on the word 'Stop!' gather the children together to look at the pictures and tell the Christmas story.

❊ ✳ ❊

— Party hat game —

You will need:

Party hats

This game works well with a large group of children (and adults). Five children stand in a row in front of the rest of the group. Each child wears a different party hat. While the rest of the group close their eyes (no peeking!), two of the children in the row swap their hats.

The children open their eyes and have to say whose hats have been swapped.

Creative ideas for worship at home

Advent is a time when Christians look forward to the coming of Christ. The family can prepare for the nativity by taking part in various activities or acts of worship in the home, aimed at bringing out the religious significance of the feast, which is so often lost through the materialism of the pre-Christmas period.

Such activities and worship can usefully include making Advent wreaths or rings and special Christmas tree decorations with a religious meaning, or holding Advent services in the home, which look forward, through readings and prayers, to both the first and second comings of Jesus Christ.

— Advent and the family wreath —

You will need:

An oasis wreath ring (obtainable in a variety of sizes); a base for the ring to stand on; four large coloured candles (either three purple and one pink, or four red); one white candle for Christmas Day; candle holders for the wreath (five flowerpots filled with sand or soil); sprigs of greenery (holly and fir or yew); secateurs; silk flowers; fir cones (wired) and decorations as required; ribbon

The Advent wreath is an old German custom that is being used to an increasing extent throughout the Western world. Wreaths can be bought, but a family should preferably make its own wreath, as we tend to give greater value to things that have been made with our own effort and thought. Also, children generally enjoy making these things.

There are many ways to make Advent rings or wreaths. Bases are available in florists' shops and garden centres and can be made of wire, straw, twigs or oasis, but the instructions below refer to oasis. Before you start to make a ring or wreath, decide how the candles are going to be fixed to the base. Obviously, candles that fall over are dangerous! One way is to use small flowerpots filled with sand or soil. The candles can be pushed into the filling quite safely. While the wreath is being made, the Christian symbolism of light can be explained to the children. Talk about how Christians have always thought of Christ as bringing light into the darkness and chaos of a disordered world.

Making the wreath

Soak the oasis ring in water for a couple of hours until it is really wet. Place the candle holders around the ring and insert the candles. Arrange the greenery around the ring, cutting to fit. Start from the outside edge and work towards the middle. Add any decorations as required.

The wreath can be decorated with purple ribbon during Advent, changed to red ribbon for Christmas Day.

Each Sunday in Advent, the family can gather around their wreath and have a little ceremony. A candle is lit or light turned on to symbolise the coming of the fullness of light; each week, an additional candle is lit.

First Sunday

After the candle is lit…

Leader: We light this first candle to remind us of all God's people, always preparing for Jesus to come among them.

Reproduced with permission from *Creative Ideas for Advent and Christmas* published by BRF 2011 (978 1 84101 856 0) www.barnabasinchurches.org.uk

All: He will teach us his ways, so that we may walk in his paths!

Leader: Jesus says, 'Be alert! You don't know when the master of the house will come back.'

All: Lord, help us to be ready to serve you, to follow you and to know you, so that our lives will reflect your love.

Second Sunday

After the candles are lit…

Leader: We light this second candle to remind us of God's word through the prophets and in the Bible, looking to the day of Jesus' birth.

All: We believe that everything written in the past was written to teach us, so that through endurance and the encouragement of the scriptures we might have hope.

Leader: I pray that God, who gives hope, will bless you with complete happiness and peace because of your faith. And may the power of the Holy Spirit fill you with hope.

All: Lord, help our lives and the whole earth to be full of the knowledge of the Lord as the waters cover the sea!

Third Sunday

After the candles are lit…

Leader: We light this third candle to remind us of John the Baptist, prophet of the most high God, who prepared the way for Jesus to come.

All: But how will we know? What does the scripture say?

Leader: God had said in the book written by Isaiah the
         prophet, 'I am sending my messenger to get the way
         ready for you.'

All: Lord, help us to be patient and stand firm, because
         the Lord's coming is near!

Fourth Sunday

After the candles are lit…

Leader: We light this fourth candle to remind us of Jesus'
         mother, Mary, and earthly father, Joseph, who believed
         God's promise: 'Mary will become pregnant and give
         birth to a son, and you will name him Jesus.'

All: May our hearts, too, praise the Lord and rejoice in
         God as our Saviour.

Leader: The angel said, 'Joseph, the baby that Mary will have
         is from the Holy Spirit. Go ahead and marry her.
         Then, after her baby is born, name him Jesus.'

All: Lord, help us to believe that you can do great things
         through people like us, too. Fill us with your Holy
         Spirit, assure us of your love and strengthen us in
         your service.

Christmas Day

After the candles are lit…

Leader: We light this fifth candle to remind us of Jesus, the
         living Word sent down to the earth!

Reproduced with permission from *Creative Ideas for Advent and Christmas* published by BRF 2011 (978 1 84101 856 0) www.barnabasinchurches.org.uk

All: What a beautiful sight! On the mountains a messenger announces to Jerusalem, 'Good news! You're saved. There will be peace.'

Leader: A child has been born for us. We have been given a son who will be our ruler.

All: His names will be Wonderful Adviser and Mighty God, Eternal Father and Prince of Peace.

Leader: Those who walked in the dark have seen a bright light.

All: The light keeps shining in the dark, and darkness has never put it out.

Leader: The Word became a human being and lived here with us.

All: From him all the kindness and all the truth of God have come down to us.

MARK 13:35; ROMANS 15:13; MARK 1:2; MATTHEW 1:20–21A; ISAIAH 52:7; 9:6A, 6B; 9:2A; JOHN 1:5, 14A, 14B

— Jesse tree —

Using a Jesse tree during the Advent season is a great way to show and tell the story of the coming of the promised Saviour, Jesus Christ.

Jesse trees date back to the Middle Ages and were inspired by Isaiah 11:1: 'Like a branch that sprouts from a stump, someone from David's family [Jesse's family] will some day be king.' Jesse was King David's father. In Matthew 1:1–17, Jesus' family tree is traced back from King David to Abraham.

A Jesse tree can be made by hanging ornaments on to a tree branch, sewing fabric ornaments on to a banner, or hanging ornaments onto a traditional Christmas tree. Jesse tree ornaments trace the ancestors and events in the Bible from creation through to the nativity.

A Jesse tree can be used as an Advent calendar at home, with the appropriate Bible passage being read each day or evening throughout Advent and then the corresponding ornament being hung on the tree.

In church, the Jesse tree can be used by concentrating on a different theme for each of the four Sundays of Advent: the Jesse tree; God's people; prophecy; people at Jesus' birth.

Ideas for symbols for an Advent Jesse tree

Creation	Genesis 1:1—2:2	World, sun, stars, animals, plants
Fall and promise	Genesis 3:1–15	Tree with fruit, serpent
Noah	Genesis 6:9—9:17	Ark, rainbow, dove, olive branch
Abraham	Genesis 12:1–5	Shepherd's crook
Abraham	Genesis 13:14–18	Oak tree
Isaac	Genesis 22:1–19	Donkey, bundles of sticks, altar, ram
Jacob	Genesis 28:10–18	Ladder, angel, stone
Joseph	Genesis 37:2–36	Coloured coat
Moses	Exodus 2:1—20:26	Basket, burning bush, commandments
Joshua	Joshua 6:1–21	Trumpets
Ruth	Ruth 1:1–22	Wheatsheaf
David	1 Samuel 16:1—18:10	Horn of oil, sling, harp
David	2 Samuel 7:8–16	Crown, six-pointed star
Solomon	1 Kings 3:2–15	Heart
Solomon	1 Kings 8:1–19	Temple

Judith	Judith 9—11	Mirror, knife
Isaiah	Isaiah 1:1–6, 16–20	Scroll, red and white wool
Jeremiah	Jeremiah 1:1–10	Hand touching mouth
Jeremiah	Jeremiah 31:31–34	Love
Ezekiel	Ezekiel 11:17–21	Heart
Daniel	Daniel 3:19–25; 6:11–28	Lion, three men in a fire
Gabriel	Luke 1:11, 19, 26–29	Angel, trumpet
Zechariah	Luke 1:5–25, 57–66	Smoking incense, sealed lips
Elizabeth	Luke 1:39–45	Elderly woman with a baby
John the Baptist	Matthew 11:7–15	Desert, locusts, honey
Joseph	Matthew 1:18–25	Carpenter's tools
Mary	Mark 3:31–35	Young woman with a baby
Jesus	Luke 2:1–7	Crib or manger, cross
Shepherd	Luke 2:8–20	Shepherd's crook, lamb
Wise men	Matthew 2:1–12	Gifts, star, camel
Simeon and Anna	Luke 2:22–38	Elderly couple

※ ✱ ※

— The crib —

The first Christmas crib is attributed to St Francis of Assisi and was created in the year 1223. Francis made a wooden manger that he surrounded with live animals on Christmas Eve. People from the town visited the crib, where they heard the story of Jesus and sang carols in praise of his birth. Francis intended to use the crib as a way of teaching people about the birth of Jesus and as something to look at and admire.

Most churches and cathedrals have a large crib during the season of Christmas and it is a lovely thing to have at home, too. Cribs are readily available in shops during the run-up to Christmas, but it's easy to make one at home using scraps of fabric, pipe cleaners and cardboard tubes.

The crib could be set up on Christmas Eve or begun a few days earlier, adding one character each evening. Finish by putting the baby Jesus in on Christmas Eve or Christmas morning. The wise men can travel towards the crib for the next twelve days along the mantelpiece, across bookcases and along the sideboard, following the star until arriving at the crib on 6 January, the feast of the Epiphany.

Blessing of the crib

When you have finished arranging the crib and figures, you may like to use the following prayer.

O Lord,
as we gather around this crib,
may we be reminded of the first Christmas
when Jesus was born in Bethlehem.
Be with us and those whom we love and care for,
this Christmas and for ever.
Amen

Finish by singing a Christmas carol such as 'Away in a manger' or 'O little town of Bethlehem'.

❄ ✱ ❄

— Stir up Sunday —

The last Sunday of the Church's year (the Sunday before Advent begins) is sometimes called 'Stir up Sunday' because of the traditional words in the special prayer for the day (the Collect):

Stir up, we beseech thee, O Lord,
the wills of thy faithful people;
that they, plenteously bringing forth the fruit of good works,
may of thee be plenteously rewarded;
through Jesus Christ our Lord.
Amen
BOOK OF COMMON PRAYER

Stir up Sunday became the traditional day for families to make their Christmas pudding. They would return from church and give the pudding its traditional lucky stir. The pudding mixture was stirred with a wooden spoon as a reminder that baby Jesus was laid in a manger made of wood, and it was stirred from east to west (clockwise) in honour of the wise men who travelled from the east to visit baby Jesus. While stirring the mixture, each family member would make a secret wish. A coin was also added to the mixture and cooked in the pudding. This was supposed to bring wealth to whoever found it on their plate on Christmas Day.

On their way back from church, children would often chant this rhyme:

Stir up, we beseech thee, the pudding in the pot;
And when we get home we'll eat the lot!

A Christmas pudding is traditionally made with 13 ingredients to represent Jesus and his twelve disciples.

Why not revive the tradition in your family and make a Christmas pudding on Stir up Sunday? Make sure you have all the ingredients and utensils and enough time to cook the pudding, then gather the family together for a great stir up! Say the Collect as you're making the pudding and discuss with your children what it might mean. Wonder with the children if, perhaps, we should try harder to do what God wants us to do. Ask the children to try to think of a new prayer for Stir up Sunday.

Let every member of the family have a stir of the mixture and make their secret wishes before the pudding is put into the basin to steam.

Perhaps you could get out a large map of the world to see where all the ingredients used in the pudding come from, and say a prayer of thanks for all those who helped to produce the ingredients.

Christmas pudding recipe

You will need:

- 225g (8oz) golden caster sugar
- 225g (8oz) suet (beef or vegetarian)
- 340g (12oz) sultanas
- 340g (12oz) raisins
- 225g (8oz) currants
- 120g (4oz) chopped candied peel
- 120g (4oz) plain flour
- 120g (4oz) fresh white breadcrumbs
- 60g (2oz) flaked almonds
- Zest of 1 lemon
- 5 eggs, beaten
- 3 level tsp mixed spice
- 150ml (5fl oz) brandy or rum (or milk)

Method

1. Mix together all the dry ingredients. Stir in the eggs and brandy and mix well. Turn the mix into four 1-pint or two 2-pint lightly greased pudding basins. Put a circle of baking parchment and foil over the top of each basin and tie securely with string. Make a string handle from one side of the basin so that it's easier to pick the basin out of the pan after cooking.

2. Put the basins in a large steamer of boiling water and cover with a lid. Simmer for 5–6 hours, topping up with boiling water from time to time if necessary.

3. If you don't have a steamer, put the basins in a large pan with inverted saucers on the base of the pan. Pour in boiling water to come a third of the way up the sides of the pudding bowls. Cover and steam as before.

4. At the end of the cooking time, remove the puddings from the pan. Cool and then change the baking parchment and foil covers for fresh ones and tie up as before. Store in a cool cupboard and serve on Christmas Day. To serve the pudding on Christmas Day, steam for two hours and serve with brandy butter, rum sauce, cream or custard.

❄ ✹ ❄

— The journey to Bethlehem —

You will need:

A map of Israel showing Nazareth and Bethlehem; pictures of swaddling clothes; a babygro or similar clothes that a new baby would wear today

We often talk about Mary and Joseph travelling to Bethlehem from Nazareth (Luke 2:4), and we usually think of Mary riding on a donkey, but it was not an easy journey to make.

If Mary and Joseph had travelled from Nazareth (in Galilee) to

Bethlehem (in Judea) in a straight line, the distance would have been about 80 miles. However, to do this they would have had to travel through Samaria, and it was dangerous to travel through Samaria if you weren't a Samaritan. A lone traveller would have been at risk of attack. Therefore, Mary and Joseph would probably have had to travel east, crossing into modern-day Jordan and then making their way down the eastern bank of the River Jordan before crossing back into Judea. This is a much longer journey.

Although the Bible doesn't mention it, tradition says that Mary travelled on a donkey while Joseph walked. A man by himself, leading a donkey, could probably have covered 20 miles a day, but, as Mary was heavily pregnant, it probably took them at least a week to make the journey.

As there were a lot of people travelling to Bethlehem for the census, Joseph and Mary may have been able to join with fellow travellers in a caravan. It would have been much safer to travel with other people and would have been more fun. A caravan would have been able to travel through Samaria, reducing the travelling time to four or five days.

With your children, talk about the excitement of preparing for the arrival of a new baby. Perhaps you know someone who has just had a baby or is expecting one. Perhaps the children could think of all the things a new mum might need for her new baby.

Tell the children that you are going to read the beginning of the Christmas story (Luke 2:1–7) and explain that Joseph had to go to Bethlehem to pay his taxes and be registered for the census. Get out a map of Israel, look at the locations of Nazareth and Bethlehem and work out the distance between them. Then think of a place that is 80 miles from where you live and ask the children if they can imagine walking that far with no roads, just dusty pathways full of thorn bushes and sharp stones. We don't know whether it was cold or warm, but what would Mary have wanted to pack for the journey? Lots of water? Bread and fruit? Perhaps Joseph would have had a stick to help him when walking.

Wonder about where they would have slept—in the open?

As you read the Bible story, ask the children to imagine Joseph, footsore and weary, going around Bethlehem knocking on doors until he found an innkeeper who saw how tired Mary was and offered them his stable to sleep in. Make sure that the children know what a stable is and that it wasn't a very suitable place for a baby to be born in. Ask the children if they know where mothers usually go these days to have a baby.

Ask the children to imagine how Mary might describe her journey.

Look at pictures of the type of baby clothes Mary would have had for baby Jesus, and compare them to the clothes a new baby wears today.

You may like to make a 'Welcome to the new baby' card to welcome Jesus into the world.

Say this prayer together:

Bless us, O Lord,
as we follow the star to Bethlehem this Christmas.
Bless us as we remember baby Jesus,
Mary, his mother, Joseph, his earthly father,
the shepherds in the fields with their sheep
and the angels who sang out the news of Jesus' birth.
Bless us as we travel in our hearts and minds
to the stable and the first Christmas. Amen

❋ ✱ ❋

— Crib service —

This simple retelling of the Christmas story is told as 'good news' and 'bad news'. Nativity figures can be placed to make a crib scene, or family members could make a tableau. If you are ambitious and have someone who can play a musical instrument, you could ask everyone for suggestions of some favourite carols after the story has been told, in which case it would be useful to have a selection to choose from.

Everyone gathers together around an empty crib scene. The figures are to hand, ready to be placed in the scene as the story is told. If real people are to make a tableau, this is created as each reading is read. The readings could be read by older members of the family while the figures are placed, or the story can be acted out in mime by younger members.

To start the proceedings, a carol such as 'Once in royal David's city' could be sung.

First reader: 'Good news!' says the angel to a girl named Mary. 'God is sending someone special into the world. His name will be Jesus. God wants you to be his mother.'

Second reader: 'Bad news!' sighs Joseph to Mary. 'The rulers of our country want to count us. That means a trip all the way from Nazareth to Bethlehem.'

Suggested carol: O little town of Bethlehem

Placing the figures: Mary and Joseph go to Bethlehem but do not enter the stable.

First reader: 'Bad news!' sighed the innkeeper. 'There's not one room left in Bethlehem. Why don't you spend the night in my stable?'

Placing the figures: Mary and Joseph enter the stable.

Second reader: 'Good news!' smiles Joseph, handing the baby to Mary. 'It's a boy, just as God promised—God's own Son, Jesus.'

Placing the figures: Baby Jesus is placed in the manger.

Suggested carol: Away in a manger

First reader: 'Good news!' calls the angel to the shepherds on the hill. 'God has sent someone special into the world. If you hurry to Bethlehem you can see him for yourselves.' Then the angels fill the sky with a good news song.

Placing the figures: The shepherds and sheep go to the stable.

Suggested carol: While shepherds watched

Second reader: 'Good news!' says Balthazar to Melchior. 'There's a new, bright star shining in the sky. It's time to pack our saddle bags and follow it. Let's see where it leads us.' And the wise men start on their journey from the far east.

Placing the figures: The wise men start their journey.

Suggested carol: We three kings

Everyone says the Lord's Prayer together.

Suggested carol: O come, all ye faithful

❄ ✱ ❄

— Twelve days —

Most people know the familiar song that starts, 'On the first day of Christmas my true love sent to me a partridge in a pear tree' and continues by adding an assortment of gifts each day until finally arriving at the twelfth day of Christmas.

There has been some discussion over the years as to the meaning of this song, and a popular theory is that it dates back to the time when Roman Catholics in Britain were not permitted to practise their faith openly (1558–1829). The song was written as a way of teaching young Catholics, and had a secret meaning known only to their church. Each gift in the carol includes a code word for a religious reality, which the children could remember.

To extend the family time together beyond Christmas Day itself, make a mobile of the twelve days of Christmas, adding another element each day.

Mobiles can be made from three basic shapes:

- A straight rod (wood or wire)
- A triangle (wire coat hanger)
- A circle of stiff card or small hula hoop covered with foil

Lengths of wooden dowelling are light and easy to glue together. Strong thread should be used to suspend the mobile from the ceiling, but light thread can be used to suspend each set of objects. The shapes should be hung at different lengths.

This is quite a big task and is ideal for lots of family members to join in with over the Christmas holiday. It may require a bit of patience to get the mobile's balance just right.

Draw the shapes for the objects on light card and decorate them using a variety of materials—sequins, feathers, glitter, leftover Christmas wrapping and unused Christmas decorations.

Draw an object each day, using the wording of the traditional song below, and then talk together about the hidden meaning in the second list below, as you hang the shape on the mobile.

On the twelfth day of Christmas, my true love sent to me
Twelve drummers drumming
Eleven pipers piping
Ten lords a-leaping
Nine ladies dancing
Eight maids a-milking
Seven swans a-swimming
Six geese a-laying
Five gold rings
Four colley birds
Three French hens
Two turtle doves
And a partridge in a pear tree!

- The 'true love' of the song refers to God.
- The partridge in a pear tree was Jesus Christ.
- Two turtle doves were the Old and New Testaments.
- Three French hens stood for faith, hope and love.
- The four colley birds were the four Gospels of Matthew, Mark, Luke and John.
- The five gold rings recalled the Torah or law, the first five books of the Old Testament.
- The six geese a-laying stood for the six days of creation.
- The seven swans a-swimming represented the seven gifts of the Holy Spirit: prophecy, service, teaching, encouragement, giving to others, leadership and mercy.
- The eight maids a-milking were the eight Beatitudes.
- The nine ladies dancing were the nine fruits of the Holy Spirit: love, joy, peace, patience, kindness, goodness, faithfulness, gentleness and self-control.

- The ten lords a-leaping were the Ten Commandments.
- The eleven pipers piping stood for the eleven faithful disciples.
- The twelve drummers drumming symbolised the twelve points of belief in the Apostles' Creed.

✳

Creative ideas for special saints

— St Nicholas' Day —

The Feast of St Nicholas is kept on 6 December. St Nicholas was a bishop in the fourth century in Myra, Asia Minor (Turkey). He is the patron saint of children, sailors and pawnbrokers. Legend says that he helped three girls to get married by providing dowries of three bags of gold for them.

In some parts of Europe (Holland, for example), Father Christmas does not visit children's homes on Christmas Eve. Instead, on his feast day, 6 December, St Nicholas (accompanied by Black Peter) leaves gifts in the children's shoes.

You could fill the children's shoes with sweets and straw before they get up in the morning and tell them the story of St Nicholas.

Spicy biscuits are traditionally eaten on St Nicholas' Day, and these could be made in the shape of St Nicholas or a bishop.

You will need:

- 400g (14oz) plain flour
- 3 level tsp baking powder
- 250g (12oz) granulated sugar
- 2 eggs
- 6 tbsp milk
- A pinch each of ginger, ground cloves, nutmeg, white pepper
- 1 tsp cinnamon
- 25g (1oz) ground almonds
- 15g (1/2oz) candied lemon, chopped into tiny pieces

- Rolling pin
- Greased baking tray

Method

1. Heat the oven to 175C, 350F, gas mark 4.
2. Mix the flour and baking powder together, make a hollow in the middle and add the eggs, sugar, milk and spices. Mix together using a fork.
3. Add the rest of the ingredients and knead to a smooth dough.
4. Sprinkle some flour on to a rolling pin and a clean surface and roll out the dough until it is about 1cm thick.
5. Cut out the shapes you want and place them on the baking tray.
6. Bake for about 20 minutes.
7. Decorate with coloured icing if you wish.

Before eating the biscuits, say a prayer about St Nicholas:

Father God,
we thank you for St Nicholas
whom we particularly remember today.
Thank you that he was always considerate
and thought of the needs of others.
Please help us, too,
to try to put other people's needs first.
Amen

❄ ✳ ❄

— St Lucia's Day —

St Lucia's Day falls on 13 December and is a winter festival of lights and candles. It is celebrated particularly in Sweden but is becoming better known in the rest of Europe, too. The Swedish church in London has a huge celebration for St Lucia every year.

St Lucia was a young Sicilian girl who died for her Christian beliefs in the fourth century. Her name means 'light'. In Sweden, a young girl dressed in white with a crown of candles brings coffee and cake to members of her family as they wake in the morning.

Saffron buns are traditionally brought by St Lucia and these are readily available in supermarkets. If you have time, you may like to gather together in the morning for coffee and saffron buns, saying this special prayer for St Lucia together. Otherwise, you may like to gather together at tea time to share them.

Father God,
as we remember St Lucia
and celebrate at this time of year,
when the nights are long and the days are short,
may the light that Jesus brought into the world
shine through us
and be seen by others in our lives.
Amen

Sample liturgy for a service following Posada

The people carrying the Posada figures gather at the back of the church, ready to bring the figures forward to the stable (which has been set up as a focal point) at the appropriate time.

Welcome

Leader: Today we celebrate as the travelling figures of Mary and Joseph arrive at their destination; we remember Jesus and the story of his birth.

Light the candles on the Advent wreath, if you have one.

The following song may be sung (to the tune of 'Twinkle, twinkle little star').

Candles, candles standing tall,
Jesus' love is for us all.
See them standing very fine,
Now we're going to make them shine.

(Light the candles.)

Candles, candles burning bright
Jesus is the world's true light.

Leader: Jesus Christ is the light for the world.
All: Jesus is our way.

Leader: With Jesus, even dark places are light.
All: Jesus is the truth.
Leader: In Jesus we shall live for ever.
All: Jesus is our life.

Carol: Come and sing the Christmas story

Reading: Luke 2:1–7

Carol: O little town of Bethlehem

The leader moves to the stable scene and the children are invited to gather around it if possible.

Leader: This is the stable in Bethlehem—the only space that could be found in the town that night.

The Posada figures are brought to the stable.

Leader: This is Joseph, the husband of Mary, who had to travel to Bethlehem to be counted and pay his taxes.

Place Joseph in the stable.

Leader: This is Mary, the mother of Jesus, who had to travel to Bethlehem with Joseph.

Place Mary in the stable.

Leader: This is the donkey that helped Mary on her journey to Bethlehem. Mary got tired because her baby was due, and rode on the donkey sometimes.

Place the donkey in the stable.

Leader: This is the baby Jesus, who was born in a stable in
Bethlehem and laid in a manger.

Place baby Jesus in the manger.

Leader: These are the people of… [name the place], who have
come to celebrate the birth of Jesus, who was born in
a stable in Bethlehem and laid in a manger.

Include the whole congregation with a gesture of the arms.

Leader: Father God,
Bless us, our homes and our families
as we remember the journey to Bethlehem,
where Jesus was born in a stable
because there was no other room available that night.
Amen

Carol: Away in a manger or Infant holy, infant lowly

Intercessions

Leader: On this happy day, we welcome Jesus into our lives.
We pray for everyone involved with the church and all
who inspire and teach us. Let your light shine.
All: And show us your glory.
Leader: We pray for our world and that we can look after it.
Let your light shine.
All: And show us your glory.

Leader: We pray for the hungry and homeless of the world. May we find ways to share the earth's harvest so that everyone has enough food and shelter. Let your light shine.

All: And show us your glory.

Leader: We pray for our families and loved ones, our friends and neighbours. Let your light shine.

All: And show us your glory.

Leader: We pray for those who are ill or mourning the loss of a loved one, which is especially hard at this time of year. Let your light shine.

All: And show us your glory.

Leader: We give thanks for all God's goodness to us, and for the birth of Jesus.

All: Amen

Carol: O come, all ye faithful

Blessing

Leader: Lord, bless everyone who looks at this stable.
May it remind us of the humble birth of Jesus
and help us think of him
who is our Saviour.
Amen

NB: The carols are only suggestions and can be replaced with others of your choice.

Sample liturgy for blessing the crib

The crib scene as we know it today owes its origins to St Francis of Assisi. In 1223 he set up a scene with Mary, Joseph, baby Jesus, shepherds, angels and kings, not forgetting the ox and the ass. This proved to be very popular and is now familiar across the world.

If the crib is not set up and blessed during a crib service, the blessing of the crib can be inserted into a carol service or other service on Christmas Eve or at the midnight service that starts Christmas Day.

At an appropriate part of the service, the leader moves to the crib and the congregation turns towards it. While this is taking place, a hymn can be sung.

Hymn: Infant holy, infant lowly

Leader: Father God, your Son Jesus came to live among us as a sign of your love for us. This crib is a symbol of his birth and of his sharing our humanity.

May we, and all who look at this crib this Christmas tide, find here a sense of hope and encouragement.

Let this crib be a reminder that we are all one great human family.

Let us bless this crib and all who pause here in the name of the Father and of the Son and of the Holy Spirit. Amen

Reproduced with permission from *Creative Ideas for Advent and Christmas* published by BRF 2011 (978 1 84101 856 0) www.barnabasinchurches.org.uk

All: Loving God, bless us and everyone who looks at this crib. May it remind us of the humble birth of Jesus and help us to think of him who is our Saviour. Amen

Carol: Away in a manger

NB: The carols are only suggestions and can be replaced with others of your choice.

Sample liturgy for a crib service

Nativity figures can be arranged in the stable during this service by carrying them up during the carol after the appropriate reading. The kings may be placed a little way away from the stable, just starting on their journey. Children could be dressed up as the characters and make a tableau during the service

Welcome

Leader: Let us thank God for that very first Christmas, which we can celebrate every year.

Light the candles on the Advent wreath, if you have one.

The following song may be sung (to the tune of 'Twinkle, twinkle, little star').

Candles, candles standing tall,
Jesus' love is for us all.
See them standing very fine,
Now we're going to make them shine.

(Light the candles.)

Candles, candles burning bright,
Jesus is the world's true light.

Carol: Come and join the celebration

Reading: God sent the angel Gabriel to the town of Nazareth in Galilee with a message for Mary… She was engaged to Joseph from the family of King David. The angel greeted Mary and said, 'You are truly blessed! The Lord is with you.' Mary was confused by the angel's words… Then the angel told Mary, 'Don't be afraid! God is pleased with you, and you will have a son. His name will be Jesus. He will be great and will be called the Son of God Most High…' Mary asked the angel, 'How can this happen? I am not married!' The angel answered, 'The Holy Spirit will come down to you, and God's power will come over you. So your child will be called the holy Son of God…' Mary said, 'I am the Lord's servant! Let it happen as you have said.' And the angel left her. *(Luke 1:26–38)*

Carol: Joy to the world

Reading: Emperor Augustus gave orders for the names of all the people to be listed in record books… Everyone had to go to their own home town to be listed. So Joseph had to leave Nazareth in Galilee and go to Bethlehem in Judea… Mary was engaged to Joseph and travelled with him to Bethlehem. She was soon going to have a baby, and while they were there, she gave birth to her firstborn son. She dressed him in baby clothes and laid him on a bed of hay, because there was no room for them in the inn. *(Luke 2:1–7)*

Carol: Away in a manger

Reproduced with permission from *Creative Ideas for Advent and Christmas* published by BRF 2011 (978 1 84101 856 0) www.barnabasinchurches.org.uk

Reading: That night in the fields near Bethlehem some
shepherds were guarding their sheep. All at once an
angel came down to them from the Lord, and the
brightness of the Lord's glory flashed around them.
The shepherds were frightened. But the angel said,
'Don't be afraid! I have good news for you, which
will make everyone happy. This very day in King
David's home town a Saviour was born for you. He
is Christ the Lord. You will know who he is, because
you will find him dressed in baby clothes and lying
on a bed of hay.' Suddenly many other angels came
down from heaven and joined in praising God.
They said, 'Praise God in heaven! Peace on earth to
everyone who pleases God.' After the angels had left
and gone back to heaven, the shepherds… hurried
off and found Mary and Joseph, and they saw the
baby lying on a bed of hay. *(Luke 2:8–16)*

Carol: See him lying on a bed of straw

Reading: Some wise men from the east came to Jerusalem
and said, 'Where is the child born to be king of
the Jews? We saw his star in the east and have
come to worship him.' … Herod told them, 'Go
to Bethlehem and search carefully for the child. As
soon as you find him, let me know. I want to go and
worship him too.' The wise men listened to what the
king said and then left. And the star they had seen in
the east went on ahead of them until it stopped over
the place where the child was. They were thrilled

and excited to see the star. When the men went into the house and saw the child with Mary, his mother, they knelt down and worshipped him. They took out their gifts of gold, frankincense and myrrh and gave them to him. *(Matthew 2:1–2, 8–11)*

Carol: O little town of Bethlehem

Leader: Thank you, God, for Jesus, your very best gift to all of us.

All: Thank you, God, for Jesus.

Leader: For Jesus, more precious than gold, frankincense and myrrh.

All: Thank you, God, for Jesus.

Leader: For the gift of Jesus, our Lord and our King.

All ·   Thank you, God, for Jesus. Amen

Carol: O come, all ye faithful

Leader: Father God, thank you for the gift of your Son, Jesus. This Christmas, help us to remember those who may not have as many presents as us and may not have a warm house to live in. Thank you for all that we have. Amen

NB: The carols are only suggestions and can be replaced with others of your choice.

Advent purse template

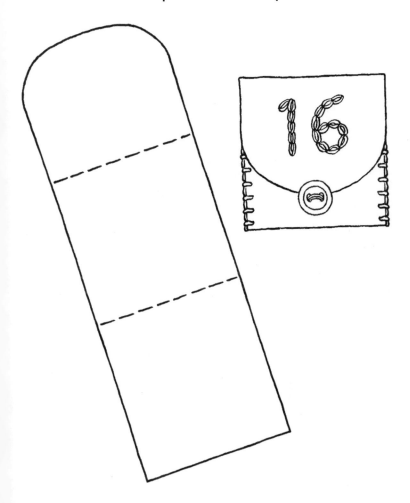

Star templates

Holly leaf template

Angel template

Christmas tree template

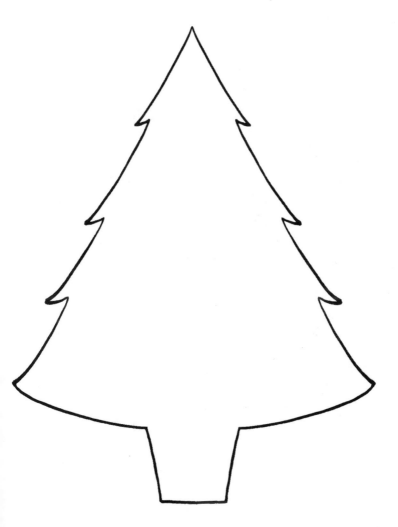

Christmas box template

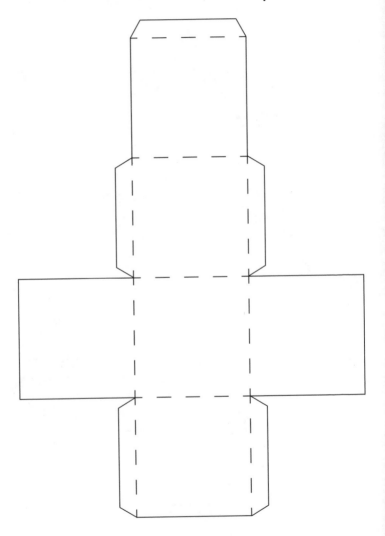

✳

Circle stars template

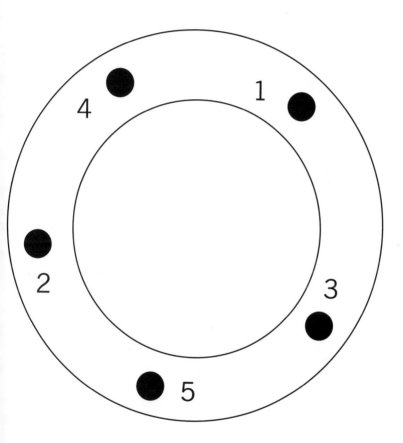

✴

How to make a piñata

A piñata is a brightly coloured clay pot, filled with tiny presents and sweets. It is hung up and then broken by the children. In Mexico, this usually happens on Christmas Day.

Here are three ways to make a piñata.

- Tape together two small shallow plastic bowls. Individual yoghurt pots or dessert containers are ideal. Wire wool can be used to erase the product design.
- Separate one unit from a cardboard egg box, leaving the hinge in place. Cut down to form a neat shape and cover the outside with pieces of white paper. Tape the two halves together.
- If you have plenty of time, cover a balloon with papier mâché, leaving a gap around the middle so that you can tape the two halves together when they are dry.
- Piñatas made from card and crêpe paper are often available in shops during the Christmas season.

Remember to enclose small wrapped sweets in the piñatas before taping the halves together. The piñatas can then be decorated with Christmas motifs using paint, colouring materials or sticky paper. Once completed, they can be hung up in the party room or on a Christmas tree.

About

BRF is a registered charity and also a limited company, and has been in existence since 1922. Through all that we do—producing resources, providing training, working face-to-face with adults and children, and via the web—we work to resource individuals and church communities in their Christian discipleship through the Bible, prayer and worship.

Our Barnabas children's team works with primary schools and churches to help children under 11, and the adults who work with them, to explore Christianity creatively and to bring the Bible alive.

To find out more about BRF and its core activities and ministries, visit:

www.brf.org.uk
www.brfonline.org.uk
www.biblereadingnotes.org.uk
www.barnabasinschools.org.uk
www.barnabasinchurches.org.uk
www.faithinhomes.org.uk
www.messychurch.org.uk
www.foundations21.org.uk

If you have any questions about BRF and our work, please email us at

enquiries@brf.org.uk

enter